Walnut Grove Hits Home:
PRAIRIE VALUES FOR THE MODERN FAMILY

"The general lessons of the script are still so important today."
-PAMELA ROYLANCE "Sarah Carter," Little House on the Prairie

"Walnut Grove Hits Home: Prairie Values for the Modern Family is a good educational tool!"
-BONNIE BARTLETT "Grace Edwards," Little House on the Prairie

"Nothing could compare to the family atmosphere on the set of Little House on the Prairie."
-WENDI LOU LEE "Baby Grace," Little House on the Prairie

"Michael Landon made us all look our best . . . He gave each actor what they needed to do their best. The legacy of Little House . . . I feel incredibly lucky to have been in this show."
-RADAMES PERA "John Sanderson," Little House on the Prairie

"The family values are just wonderful in that show . . . The great part is how long ago we did it, and it's so relevant today."
-TODD BRIDGES "Solomon Henry," Little House on the Prairie

Walnut Grove Hits Home:

PRAIRIE VALUES FOR THE MODERN FAMILY

Alicia Hogan Murphy

Orlando, Florida

Walnut Grove Hits Home: Prairie Values for the Modern Family

Published in the USA by
BearManor Media
1317 Edgewater Dr. #110
Orlando, FL 32804
www.BearManorMedia.com

Cover design by Lilian Rosenstreich
Cover image "Yellow Field" by Nana B. Agyei.
Cover LH icons used with permission of Bill and Jeanne Northum, Old West Miniatures

Hardcover Edition
ISBN: 978-1-62933-759-3

Table of Contents

For Michael Landon,
whose words and works are still so prevalent,
even thirty years after his passing.

Introduction

"Maybe I'm old-fashioned, but I think viewers are hungry for shows in which people say something meaningful."

—Michael Landon

In our time of modern technology, science, and medicine, it's difficult to imagine growing up as a pioneer in the 1870s. No computers, no cars, no electricity, and definitely no cell phones. *Where's the Wi-Fi?!!* These luxuries, which are right at our fingertips every single day, have become our entertainment, our pastime, and in some cases, our obsession. Television programs have progressed over time from moving silhouette images to basic black and white news broadcasts, to split-screen presidential candidate debates, to war coverage, to family shows (in color), to sit-coms, to cablevision, and now to reality TV and Netflix.

The family dramas and sit-coms of the 1970s and 1980s provided audiences with relatable tales of parents' and children's experiences navigating everyday life. One of these shows was unique in that its story was set one hundred years earlier. *Little House on the Prairie* took us back to a much simpler time: the 1870s and 1880s. Horse-drawn wagons? Lanterns? *OUTHOUSES???* The horror! We watched as the Ingalls endured every personal, social, and economic hardship possible. Yet the family we grew to know and love managed to find blessings and joy again and again because of their outlook on life; a simple life of hard work and gratitude, good morals and great faith.

I grew up watching *Little House on the Prairie* when it aired on NBC during prime time (Monday nights at 8:00!) and have been watching it in syndication since it went off the air.

My children are now growing up seeing the show and learning from it the same lessons I did.

Granted, they giggle way more often than I did (at the calico-infused clothing and hick lingo), but "I reckon" it's because they prefer their own ripped jeans and GIFs. They've also gotten so comfortable with their "prairie friends" that they now refer to "Charles" as "Chaz." Good grief.

As many times as I've seen every episode, I remain in constant awe of Michael Landon's genius. He was a brilliant writer with a creativity that was beyond superior. Writing and directing a show that dealt with serious issues such as racism, poverty, child abuse, alcoholism, prejudice, inequality, and drug abuse, Michael Landon was way ahead of his time. These issues still exist, and the show is being watched by so many today, because its themes resonate with audiences everywhere. That is why I decided to write this book. It's needed in our world right now, during these very uncertain times; we are currently making history as we live through the nightmares of a global pandemic. *Little House on the Prairie's* messages are timeless, so they'll continue to be meaningful, even after our world has found "normal" again.

Many members of the *Little House* cast agree and have offered their sentiments and memories within these pages! "The show's values are a reflection of our leader, Michael Landon," Melissa Gilbert has said. Reflecting on the impact of *Little House* on her own life, she commented, "I absorbed really important life lessons about family, community, and tolerance."

As we approach the thirtieth anniversary of Michael Landon's passing,

I wanted to honor his memory with this book. *Little House on the Prairie* instilled many lasting values in me as a child; and now, as an adult, I'm gaining useful knowledge of positive parenting by once again watching "Ma" and "Pa" raise their family. In our time of "give kids lots of choices" and "put them in Time Out when they're naughty" (insert eye roll), I have admired the respect that parents were able to command in earlier generations. Journey with me back to Walnut Grove, and discover the amazing lessons of the prairie!

Chapter 1
Admitting Our Mistakes

"Home Is the Nicest Word There Is."

THE FIRST EPISODE OF *LITTLE HOUSE ON THE PRAIRIE,* called "A Harvest of Friends," introduces us fully to the warmth of the Ingalls family and the love they share. After Pa builds their house on the banks of Plum Creek, both the parents and children are happy and grateful for the simplest things. "Wood floors . . . real glass in the windows?" says "Caroline" (Ma). "Laura" and "Mary" are thrilled to have their own room, even though it's a tiny loft with one bed and just enough space to move around. Laura is ecstatic about having her "own window!"

How many times have we heard our kids complain that they don't have the newest iPhone or the biggest house, or the most expensive sneakers, or an in-ground pool "like everyone else has?" It can be so hard to thrust upon them how important it is to find joy in what they *do* have, even the little things. How funny is it when they say, "I'm the only one of my friends who doesn't have one," and then you talk to eight other moms whose children also don't have that desired thing? The Ingalls are refreshing to watch, because their hard life – their poor life – on the prairie really reminds us that we enjoy so many luxuries today.

When "Charles" (Pa) climbs into the loft during episode one to see how his girls like their new room, Laura says, "I've decided something. Home is the nicest word there is."

One of the greatest lessons I've learned from this first episode and many others is the willingness of the parents (in this case, Charles) to admit their mistakes. Now hold on! Don't slam the book shut. I don't mean that parents should assume the responsibility of every family problem or bow down to their children whenever an issue arises. I'm saying that it's a good example for our children when we can look at a situation and admit that we could have handled it in a better way. Charles does this in "A Harvest of Friends." In order to have enough money to buy the plow he needs to plant his crop, he agrees to take two jobs in town in addition to working his farm. He estimates that it should only take him two weeks to earn the money he owes.

As the days drag on, Charles becomes more and more exhausted. When Caroline brings to his attention the fact that he has snapped at his girls several times telling them to be quiet, he goes to his daughters and says he'd like to tell them a bedtime story. His tale is about a "grumpy farmer" who gets up early every morning to stomp off to work and sometimes forgets to say goodbye to his wife and "three pretty little girls." Laura and Mary can relate to this story and are thrilled when Charles promises to take them on "the biggest, bestest picnic of all time." Charles knows he has been taking his exhaustion out on his family, and he admits it.

When parents can admit they've been wrong and apologize to their kids, it shows children the right thing to do when they make a mistake. It also makes parents human . . . which we are.

*****

The Ingalls' crop is destroyed by a tornado in the episode "Going Home" (season two). Charles, who, despite working long, hard days, is always worried about money. He decides that he's tired and tells the family it's time to sell the farm and move back to their old home in Wisconsin. Laura begs him not to give up – to keep trying – but Charles tells her he can't. He fixes up the house and barn for a couple who comes to buy the farm, but the night before the sale, he begins to have second thoughts about leaving Walnut Grove. After all, his family is happy there. They have friends there. They love the town.

"What happened to me?" Charles asks Caroline. "I just quit on this place. Now I've sold it, and it's too late. You know, I just realized something. I made the decision to sell this place all by myself. I never even asked you. So concerned about myself. I didn't even ask you . . . We'd been through a lot. *We* had. And I never even asked you. I just gave up. My own little girl told me that, and I wouldn't listen to her." Charles admits to his family that he has been selfish and hasty in making the choice to leave their home. ***Recognizing and acknowledging fault is such a powerful show of character; one we can share with our children.***

*****

Another example of this can be found in the episode "The Cheaters" (season five), where "Jonathan and Alice Garvey" are concerned about their son "Andy's" grades. He failing, and since Alice is Walnut Grove's teacher, she's feeling embarrassed by her son's lack of success in school. She decides to set up tutoring sessions with "Nellie Oleson," the meanest, most hated girl in school (but one of the best students). Nellie agrees to help Andy; she has ulterior motives, however (a pattern that weaves itself through each and every episode involving Nellie!). She cheats her way through school and tells Andy to spy on his mother at home so he can get ahold of the upcoming test questions for her. ***GASP!*** She threatens to tell on him for cheating if he doesn't deliver. ***DOUBLE GASP!***

Feeling trapped, Andy continues to cheat and provide Nellie with test material. When Laura finds out and tells Charles, he decides to take Andy fishing so they can talk. I absolutely love this scene, because ***Charles talks to Andy about the situation without lecturing him or really even saying that he knows Andy's secret.*** "Listen to those frogs ... When I was your age, there was nothin' I liked better than going night froggin.' I used to sneak out at night so I could do it. I remember one time I stayed out the whole night. Snuck back into the house, my folks were still asleep; they didn't even know I was gone. I just climbed right into bed, and they never knew a thing about it. That's not the only time I cheated as a kid. I guess all kids do. I remember I used to play hooky from school once in a while. I learned how to copy my ma's handwriting, so I'd write notes about how I was sick. The thing is, I never felt very good about it. Guilty conscience, I guess. Then one day, I just got my courage up and went and told my ma and pa. 'Tell ya, my pa gave me a whippin' I'll never forget. Ya know, I never enjoyed anything as much as that. Cleared my conscience I guess."

Andy, uncomfortable, decides that he's caught enough fish and "best be goin.' " As he turns to leave, he says, "Mr. Ingalls? . . . Thanks."

Charles' subtle, non-accusing way of helping Andy realize on his own that he should come clean really works. Great parenting technique! The boy finally cracks and tells his mother the truth in front of the entire class. Of course, she is devastated, *but kudos to Andy for his bravery!*

After his confession, Andy awaits his punishment at home. I think his parents' reactions surprise him a bit. They admit that they, too, have made mistakes: expecting too much of Andy and pairing him up with Nellie. *Amen to that! Disaster comes from* ***any*** *encounter with Nellie, let alone* ***daily*** *tutoring sessions with her.*

They praise Andy for having the courage to finally tell the truth, and though they "can't abide" stealing the tests and cheating, Alice and Jonathan admit that they also had a part in this whole thing.

"Are you ashamed of me now?" Andy asks.

"We didn't expect you to grow up without making a few mistakes," Jonathan tells him. "Everyone makes mistakes . . . We love you."

I've always loved that line: ***"We didn't expect you to grow up without making a few mistakes.*** "SO important for both kids and parents to remember.

When children can be honest with their parents without fear, they feel safe and loved. These feelings can truly make home "the nicest word there is."

During a conversation I had with Hersha Parady (Alice), she told me, "I encouraged my son to show my grandchildren "The Cheaters." ***It's definitely filled with lessons for both children and parents!***

"People would do themselves a great favor if they would take the blame for things that go wrong, and say to themselves, "I've got to do something about this . . . You can't do anything if you always blame your problems on someone else."
—Michael Landon

Chapter 2
Staying Positive and Instilling Courage in Our Kids

"Laughing and Loving Each Other . . . That's What Life's All About."

The idea of being courageous and staying positive resonates throughout *so* many *Little House* episodes. ***Instilling optimism and bravery in our children can really empower them.*** Our kids constantly look to us for direction and guidance. The way we approach life will influence how they navigate the world.

In "Child of Pain" (season one), the Ingalls try to help an alcoholic single father to overcome his addiction. Charles stays with the man at his home while Caroline and the girls invite his son, "Graham," to live with them during his father's recovery. This is a difficult time for everyone.

"How do you think your father would feel if he knew you weren't eating supper?" Caroline asks Graham.

"He wouldn't know," Graham answers matter-of-factly. "He's always drunk by suppertime." *Heartbreaking.*

Caroline allows Graham to decide when he's ready to join the family at the table, which he soon does. She shows great sensitivity to Graham's feelings, not pushing him when he's feeling angry or sad. She is also understanding when he wants to walk to school by himself (he doesn't want others to know he's staying with the Ingalls). Later, when Graham begs to go visit his pa, Caroline hugs him and says, "I'm sorry, Graham. It won't be much longer . . . You know, you and I have the same problem. You miss your pa, and I miss my husband." ***Caroline empathizes with the boy, letting him know that she understands the pain he's feeling. Her sense of compassion is infused into her own children's personalities as well, which is a fine example of how our children watch us and often model our behavior.*** Mary teaches Graham about chickens and roosters, even giving him one of her own chickens to keep. Caroline encourages his idea to build a cage for the bird. Graham really feels safe with the Ingalls as a result of the love and optimism they show to him. ***Children really do learn what they live!***

*****

The first episode of season two is called "The Richest Man in Walnut Grove." When Hanson's Mill is forced to close because a major customer declares bankruptcy, Charles doesn't receive his paycheck and is left with a ton of debt. The family must find a way to pay bills, and their infamous courage kicks in. Charles works two jobs, Caroline plows the field, Mary drops out of school temporarily to work for a seamstress in town, and Laura and Carrie do all of the chores at home. *Meanwhile, my kids are put out just by being asked to empty the dishwater. Good Lord! Raise your hand if you can relate.*

Nellie and Willie Oleson tease Laura, saying that her pa can't get a decent job, smells bad, and is only good for cleaning up after the animals. When Charles finds Laura in the barn loft crying because of those hurtful words, he tells her, "Well, they're right about two of the three. I do clean the stables, and when I get home from working all day, I don't exactly smell like a bottle of Lemon Verbena, now do I? Now as for the decent job, that's somethin' else. Any job a man can do to make his way in this world is a decent job, as long as he works hard at it and does his best. Ya know, God didn't put sweat in a man's body for no reason. He put it there so he could work hard, cleanse himself, and feel proud. Don't you ever forget that. Hard-workin' folks only smell bad to other folks who have nothing else to do but stick their noses in the air."

Charles takes a bad situation and turns it on its head. He encourages his daughter to remember never to quit or be weakened by the cruelty of others. What a sweet lesson. On her way down the ladder from the loft, Laura stops and says, "Pa? I just love you so much."

The whole family works together until they have enough money to pay their bill at the mercantile and stock up on necessities. As they pack their purchases into the wagon, town merchant "Nels Oleson" says to Charles, "That's quite a family you've got. I'd like to think that my young ones would all pull together if things got bad . . . Believe it or not, Charles, I think you're the richest man in Walnut Grove."

This episode is a great example of how love and positivity prevail. I think it's important to let our kids know that there will always be someone richer, faster, maybe even wiser . . . but they can't quit. They have to keep going. Fighting. Trying. Working for what they want. A family working together seems like the best work there could possibly be. These lessons from Michael Landon are so valuable.

I am constantly trying to emphasize to my children that families help each other and stick together. Both my dad and my father-in-law have substantial health issues, so my mom and mother-in-law need help with certain things. It's important to me that my kids lend a hand. I have said to them repeatedly, "This is what families do." I hope that idea will stay with them as they grow up . . . Meanwhile, I'm sure they wish the dishwasher would just learn to empty itself.

*****

The idea of determination and perseverance is repeated in "I'll Be Waving as You Drive Away" (season four), the famous episode where Mary loses her eyesight. She is so afraid and so angry. It would be easy for Charles and Caroline to keep her at home, where they could safely coddle her. That's what Mary wants; to sit in a chair and be angry.

Instead, her parents choose to send her away to a school for the blind, where she can be helped and taught independence. Caroline's angst while telling Mary is painful to watch.

"Mary, your pa and I have been to see Dr. Baker. He knows about a school. He thinks maybe it would be a good idea if you went there. Just for a while."

"What could *I* do at a *school*?"

"It's a school for the blind. They can teach you a lot of things there."

"Can they make me a teacher? Can they teach me to *see*?"

"Mary, it won't be for long. Just try it."

"I've never heard of one of those schools around here," Mary says suspiciously.

"It's not around here," Ma says gently. "It's in Iowa."

"Oh . . . Yeah, I understand now. You just wanna get me out from under foot."

"Mary, that's not true, and you know it."

Mary bursts into tears. "Then don't send me away. Please don't send me away. Let me stay here. Please. I don't want people looking at me, feeling sorry for me. Please let me stay. *Please* let me stay!"

"Mary, I don't *want* to send you away . . . But if they can help you . . . You can't spend the rest of your life sitting in that chair."

"WHY NOT?!" Mary screams. "Why not? Why can't I just sit here? There's nothing for me to see. It's dark. No matter where I go, all there is is darkness . . . You've already decided to send me there."

"Yes, we have," says Ma. ***She is both loving and firm at the same time.***

Caroline and Charles are doing what they know is best for their daughter, which isn't always the easiest choice. ***Because of their courage, Mary learns to be brave. She learns to make the most of her situation and never give up.***

Sometimes, as parents, we just have to follow our gut. Staying positive and making lemons into lemonade can really pay off. Things tend to find a way of working out.

"With a houseful of kids, you give each other strength."
—Michael Landon

Chapter 3
Addressing Racism and Prejudice

"Black and White are Just Two Colors."

WITH THE STORY OF *LITTLE HOUSE* taking place about twenty years following the end of the Civil War in our country, there are plenty of meaningful episodes that deal with racism and prejudice. With all that is going on in the United States today, these shows have invaluable messages!

When I was growing up in the 1970s and 80s, it was clear to me that many people in my parents' generation were still racist. I never understood why. In my mind, we were / are all created by the same maker, so we must all be equal. I heard a variety of ideas from others, both my elders and my peers, but I chose to form and keep my own opinion on this subject.

Now, as a mom, I see even more confusion in my own children, who are appalled when they hear that people mistreat each other because of a difference in skin color.

"Why does that matter to anyone?" my 11-year-old son recently said to me. "I don't care what color my friend's skin is. All that matters is that he's a nice person." *Amen.* And my daughter refers to her black friend as "my curly-haired friend." No mention or care about skin color. This makes me happy – and hopeful – knowing that perhaps the existence and tolerance of racism may come to an end with their generation.

"The Wisdom of Solomon" (season three) is a *Little House* episode with very eye-opening messages about racism. Actor Todd Bridges was absolutely *phenomenal* as "Solomon Henry," the son of former slaves, who is tired of working on the plantation. He wants to go to school. "*Who the heck would want to go to school if they didn't have to?" most kids would probably say. This is because they're focused on long days of school work followed by hours of homework, rather than on the fortune they are inheriting as they learn.* "The Wisdom of Solomon" addresses this beautifully. It begins with the young boy running toward his mother and brother in the field as he is being chased by an angry man driving a wagon. Solomon has stolen a book from the steps of the nearby school. His mother begs the man not to punish Solomon and then reprimands her son.

Solomon decides that he doesn't want to end up like his family and leaves home. Making his way to Walnut Grove, he winds up at the Ingalls' house, where he is welcomed. They decide to let Solomon stay with them so that he can go to school, and he is thrilled! The scene where Charles takes the children to school for Solomon's first day is funny. "Harriet Oleson," the town's rich bitch (and the original Beverly Goldberg) questions the boy's residency. Charles tells her, "Oh, you see, Solomon is my son from a former marriage. I know *you* understand, but a lot of people in this town wouldn't." Of course, the racist Harriet is appalled. Her reaction is hilarious!

What happens inside the schoolhouse *isn't* so hilarious. "Miss Beadle" (a.k.a. WORLD'S SWEETEST TEACHER!) asks the class to think of things they dislike. The children give answers like cleaning the chicken coop, homework, chores . . .

When Solomon is asked what he dislikes, he answers, "Bein' a n-----."

A sad silence takes over the room. *When this episode is aired now, this comment is muted, and the scene with Mrs. Oleson's funny reaction to Charles is cut out completely. Though very real and powerful, they're neither politically correct nor acceptable today.*

Charles talks to Solomon at bedtime about his remark at school. "Why'd you say it?"

"Because it's the truth. If I was white, my pa would still be alive. Being a n----- killed my pa. You'd hate somethin' that killed your papa . . . You answer me something, Sir. Would you like to live to be a hundred?"

Charles smiles. "Sure I would . . . "

"Would you rather be black and live to be a hundred, or white and live to be fifty?"

Charles is speechless. *And so am I, every time I watch this scene. Just so awful that anyone – child or adult – should have to feel that way about the color of his skin.* ***It's beautiful that Little House continues to educate us about the pain inflicted by racism, and it's wonderful that the Ingalls family loves this special little boy like he's one of their family. I wish this episode could serve as a worldwide example of acceptance.***

When I asked Todd Bridges about his thoughts and memories of playing Solomon in this episode, he answered very passionately. "One thing I loved about doing *Little House on the Prairie* was the values that Mr. Ingalls had. He wasn't racist, he was a good father, and they had a good mother for the girls. The girls were wonderful children who brought Solomon Henry, my character, onto their property to live with them. I was the one who had told them that I didn't have a family. And then my brother came to see me and said, 'Mama's missing you. You gotta go back home.' So then I realized that I could no longer lie to myself, to think that I could learn how to read and write. For a minority person in that particular time frame, it wasn't allowed. So I realized that I had to go home, and see my mom, and work the farm."

"The family values were just wonderful in that show," Todd continued. "Being able to be taken in right away was unusual for then – especially me being a black, and the others being white – but it was amazing how we all gelled together. To bring this character into the light, to make him so endearing . . . You really got attached to Solomon. He was such a good kid. He wanted to be a doctor, but when he realized he wouldn't be able to work with anyone but (Native American) Indians, he knew he had to go back home, and face his mother . . . His mother told him he wouldn't be able to learn to read and write, but he had to find out for himself."

"It was wonderful to play that character. The great part is how long ago we did it, and it's so relevant today. That family was definitely all about love, and to me that's what a family is. If you love each other, you can make anything work."

Todd recalled, "Michael Landon's character was just wonderful. He really brought it home in that scene where I was really asking questions. He had to answer them. We were trying to bring across in that show that people have to understand it doesn't matter what color you are or where you're from. What matters is that you have to learn not to judge people, not to hate people, but to just *love* them. If you can't love them, then have understanding for people. We don't know what people are going through or what they're dealing with, but the bottom line is, this country has no place for racism. I hope (people) can understand that. We need to learn to get together and unite as a country. We are Americans. And America only will be strong if *we* stay strong and if *we* have understanding . . . God bless you all, and please remember that we cannot be strong unless America starts to really unite under one flag. United we stand. Otherwise we will fall. God bless you!"

WOW! So heartfelt and enlightening. To me, Todd's words truly paint a picture of what it meant to work on this show and to really breathe in the goodness that Michael Landon created, both in the script and on set. The sense of family – and what it really means to be a family – came through week after week on Little House. I have read repeatedly that the cast and crew were like one big family, and that Michael Landon made a point of wrapping up at a certain time each day so that everyone could be home to have dinner with their real-life families.

Todd also hits home with his sentiments about the importance of ending racism in our country. I agree with him. There's simply no place for it in our land of the free and home of the brave.

*****

Also highlighting the subject of racism is the episode "Blind Journey," in which Harriet Oleson travels from the city of Winoka, Dakota, with Charles and his black friend, "Joe Kagan." They are transporting Mary, Adam, and all of the blind children to Walnut Grove, where a new blind school has been established. Because so many people are making the trip, they have to take turns walking and riding in the wagons. Charles offers Harriet a seat on Joe's wagon, and she turns it down; simply because Joe is black. She would rather walk miles and miles and miles than sit "with the likes of" Joe.

During the trip, a blind, black boy named "Samson" asks Joe why Harriet doesn't like them.

"To her, we just ain't the right color," Joe tells him. "What's the right color?"

"*Her* color ..."

"Well, what's the difference between black and white?" Samson asks.

"You never seen either one, have you?"

Samson shakes his head.

"Well, Samson," they're just two different colors, that's all. But some folks get it in their head . . . makes all the difference in the world."

"Maybe folks would be nicer to other folks," Samson says, "if they never saw anything."

"You know, Samson," Joe smiles, "You've got more vision than some folks with two eyes."

The camera pans to Charles, who is listening nearby, and then to Harriet, who has also heard the conversation. She looks ashamed.

This writing and direction here are *brilliant.*

When the entourage finally arrives at the new blind school in Walnut Grove, Harriet greets her family. Also there (and furious) is "Mr. Judd Larabee," a bigot who is angered when he sees black teacher "Hester Sue Terhune" and her black students. He marches over to Harriet and barks, "Are you out of your mind? One n----- living in Walnut Grove maybe we can accept, but-"

"Shut up!" she tells him. "Mr. Larabee, if there's one thing I cannot tolerate, it's a bigot! And you are precisely just that! A narrow-minded bigot!"

Larabee is shocked. "But you always said-"

"Never *mind* what I said!" she cuts him off. "It's what I say *now* that matters. Black and white are just two different colors. That's all! Just two different colors! And it's people like you, who have it fixed in their heads that it makes all the difference!"

The lesson here is fantastic. Skin color is just that. Color. What truly matters is a person's heart. *I really hope children today are watching the Little House reruns! The show lends itself to such meaningful and memorable conversations between kids and their parents.*

*****

Differences between black and white aren't the only races upon which the series touches. The episode "Survival" (season one) deals with issues between Native Americans and white men. The Ingalls are heading home from Mankato when they meet a U.S. Marshall named "Jim Anders." He is searching for Jack Lamehorse, a Native American (a "Renegade Sioux," as Anders describes him) who has done nothing wrong (except, according to Anders, "he got born"). When the Ingalls say they haven't seen Lamehorse, Mr. Anders tells them to "keep an eye out for that savage."

A blizzard hits as the family travels on toward home. They are forced to find shelter in an abandoned cabin. While Charles is out hunting, Mr. Anders knocks at their door. He is frostbitten and in need of help. Caroline and the girls give him food and welcome him to warm up by the fireplace. Once he is feeling better, Anders begins to load his rifle.

"Do you ever shoot people?" Laura asks him.

"Not unless I have to," he answers.

Caroline looks on with concern.

"When we saw you on the road, you were looking for an Indian," Laura continues.

"Jack Lamehorse," says Anders.

"Well, what did he do?" Laura wants to know.

"Laura, you're being a bother!" Caroline interrupts.

"It's no bother," Anders tells her. "It's history. I mean, it's something they should know, something they should learn and remember."

Caroline moves closer to her girls as Anders continues. "In '62, the Sioux just about wiped all of us out. Folks like your ma and pa, children like you . . . They almost got us. But we got up; and we fought. And we taught 'em a lesson."

Now Caroline looks more concerned about what her children are hearing.

"Well, one of their chief's name," continues Anders, "was Jack Lamehorse. He's the only one left."

"But what happened to the others?" Laura asks.

"They're dead," Anders says. "Gone. Some we shot, others we hung."

Caroline finally interjects, knowing that this kind of talk involves way more than a "lesson" about the past. It recalls brutal murder as a result of hatred and is completely inappropriate for children's ears. Caroline, in her polite but firm way, simply says, "I think that's enough history, Mr. Anders." What she doesn't tell him in words, she says with her eyes. Anders knows that he has crossed her comfort line. *While I admire how Caroline allows this hateful man to express his perception of what happened in the past, I feel she should have stopped him much sooner. His words are much too harsh and prejudiced. She does challenge him a bit more in a later scene:*

"Murderer? You keep saying that! Who did he murder??!!" Caroline is clearly exasperated with Mr. Anders, who goes off on a rant about how Lamehorse was tried and sentenced to hang, but Abraham Lincoln interfered. Caroline and Charles (silently) agree to disagree with him, knowing that there is no changing this guy's mind. *Smart. We can't control how others think or feel, but we can choose to shut down their inappropriate talk, especially when our children are within earshot.*

*****

Prejudice. A similar (if not the same) theme which threads itself through the *Little House* series as well. Many episodes tend to deal with the size of people, rather than the color of their skin. In "The Man Inside" (season five), an obese man laments his immense weight gain, which his doctors have not been able to explain. His daughter, a friend of Laura, is embarrassed to be seen with him, especially after Laura and the other kids make a rude joke about his weight. As a result, he tells his family that he's leaving town to take a new job with the railroad. He stays at the blind school, where he works to earn his keep. When he becomes very ill, the Ingalls have a hard time convincing him to have the operation necessary for his survival. He doesn't want to disgrace his family any longer. It isn't until his daughter talks to him about all of the people who love him – including herself – that he begins to fight for his life. ***This episode is a perfect example of how one hurtful comment can destroy someone's self-esteem. It's an important reminder for our children, especially because they not only have to be cautious about what comes out of their mouths, but also about what they are texting, posting, and emailing. Michael Landon and Little House were way ahead of their time with this message!***

*****

"Annabelle" (season six) has a similar lesson about prejudice. When the circus comes to Walnut Grove, Nels discovers that "the fat lady" in the side show is his sister. He hasn't seen her in years, because he has pushed her away, embarrassed of her size. She confronts him, saying, "Ya know, I have a place in this life. I was put here on this planet for a purpose; maybe not an exalted purpose, but a purpose. You know, I make people laugh! And that makes them feel good. You know, that's not a bad thing to do, Nels."

It is at this moment that Nels wakes up to what is really important. The night of the circus, in front of the entire community, he announces that

Annabelle is his sister. "You know, that's a pretty wonderful thing to be able do with your life," he says. "Make people happy.

And I am *proud* to say that one of the people who helped make you happy tonight is someone very close to my heart. My sister, Annabelle." ***The message of acceptance here is terrific. Who cares how heavy someone is if they are kind and giving and loving?***

*****

"Little Lou" is an episode of *Little House: A New Beginning* (season nine), in which a member of the circus visits Walnut Grove again; a little person named "Lou Bates." He and his wife act as clowns, and she is having a baby. It's a difficult delivery, and "Dr. Baker" cannot save the wife. Lou is left, with the help of his own mother, to take care of his new baby girl. Before she dies, his wife asks him not to work for the circus again. She wants a more normal life for their daughter.

When Lou goes into Walnut Grove to look for a job, the first person he deals with is, of course, nasty Harriet. At first, she is enchanted with Lou because she thinks he's cute. But as soon as anyone even considers hiring him, she interferes. Telling Nels that they cannot have "a midget" working in the store because "he's not like us," and threatening to close her account at the bank if Lou is hired as a teller, Harriet prevents him from being able to support his family; all because of her prejudice.

Unfortunately, Lou doesn't seem to be able to find a place in Walnut Grove until the Olesons' daughter, "Nancy," falls down a deep well, and the only adult small enough to fit down the hole is Lou. When he saves the little girl's life, Harriet finally accepts him and makes arrangements for Lou to have a job in town. Again, it's very sad that, as a good, honest, hard-working man, Lou couldn't just be welcomed into the town in the first place. This episode shows just how strong and hurtful prejudice can be. ***It's so important for us to***

emphasize to our children the importance of accepting others for who they are, not what they look like.

Every script I've written and every series I've produced
have expressed the things I most deeply believe.
—Michael Landon

Chapter 4
Dealing with Bullying

"'Turn the Other Cheek' is Easier Said Than Done . . ."

One of the hardest things for a parent to deal with is the knowledge that her child is being bullied or is bullying another. There's that very fine line between telling our kids to walk away and teaching them to fight back if someone is mistreating them. Nowadays, we also have to worry about cyber bullying. With most of their communication happening via text or various apps, our kids are at risk for a whole lot more bullying than we ever were. *Awful.* The conversations we need to have with our children and the continuous watch we must keep on their devices can be nerve-racking. Luckily for the Ingalls, they don't have to worry about such things on the prairie. They do, however, experience all the *traditional* kinds of bullying over the years.

Caroline and Laura have trouble with another mother/daughter duo right away in the second episode of the series. "Country Girls" was named so because it is the nickname given to Laura and Mary by nasty Nellie Oleson. "Country girls. Don't even know what a blackboard is!"

"Anybody in particular you liked, Laura?" Charles asks after the first day of school.

"Someone in particular I *don't* like! That snippy Nellie Oleson!"

"Laura!" Caroline scolds.

"Well, ya know what she called us?" Laura continues. "Country girls!"

Charles shrugs. "Well, ya *are* country girls. There's nothing bad about that."

"There is the way *she* said it!" Laura argues. "Look at the country girls!" she says, rolling her eyes. "Made me so mad I wanted to smack her good!"

"Now just a minute!" Charles interrupts. "I don't wanna hear you talking like that. You go to school to learn, not fight."

"Part of what you have to learn is how to get on with others," Caroline adds.

"All right," says Laura. "I'll try."

"Young lady, you're gonna do a lot more than just try," Charles insists.

"Remember Laura," Caroline reminds her, "Do unto others."

Charles continues, "That's right. And that means no name-callin,' no fightin,' and no teasin.' Understood?"

A few days later, Caroline goes into the mercantile to sell eggs. When Harriet (who has heard negative things from Nellie about Laura and Mary) sees that some of Caroline's eggs are brown, she insists that "brown eggs don't bring as much as white." She tells Caroline that she will pay four cents less for her brown eggs. Caroline is puzzled at first and then annoyed; but because her family needs the money, she accepts Harriet's price. However, when Harriet turns around and sells the brown eggs to a customer for the same price as the white, Caroline's blood boils.

She deals with this bullying very sensibly, returning to the mercantile next time with only *white* eggs.

"You didn't bring any brown eggs!" Mrs. Oleson says.

"Oh, my husband sold them to the man at Hanson's mill," Caroline answers, "for three cents more than you gave me."

"Well," Mrs. Oleson sneers, "that's gratitude."

"No, that's good business," Caroline shoots back.

"Maybe he'll take your white eggs as well."

"As a matter of fact," Caroline states pleasantly, "my husband said he'll be glad to get them. Good day, Mrs. Oleson."

Harriet scurries out from behind the counter as Caroline proudly walks away. "Now, Mrs. Ingalls, I'm a very busy woman; too busy to quibble over pennies. We'll buy your brown eggs; for the same price as the white."

Caroline smirks. She has won. *Score!* She succeeds in shutting down Harriet's bully-like behavior, and is able to do so calmly and quietly. We can teach our kids to do the same in their own lives by encouraging them to choose words and a tone that are gentle yet firm. ***Our children can learn to be respectful to those who may bully them, but at the same time demand respect in return.*** *This is a very effective way to handle such situations, especially because a bully is typically looking to break the other person down. Maintaining composure and staying matter-of-fact is a good way to turn the tables and make the bully back off.*

By the way, I have to include a short story here. My twelve-year-old daughter peeked over my shoulder while I was working on this chapter. She giggled (quite loudly) and said, "You're writing about dealing with bullies? Okay! If someone bugs you, just punch them. That's what Charles does. No need to use your words! Just haul off and hit 'em! But take your shirt off first!"

I must say that I, too, giggled at this. My girl has seen enough episodes of *Little House* to know that punching is frequently Charles' answer to bullies! NOT the lesson I wanted my kids to take from the show, but I also realize that Michael Landon, while portraying a man of solid principles and overall goodness, was also interested in impressing his audience with his strong physique and confidence. And, whenever possible, he did so without a shirt on. His brilliance strikes again!

*****

Bullying is presented in abundance throughout the episode called "The Music Box" (season three). When Laura is given a dictionary for her birthday rather than one of the fun toys she's been eyeballing in the window of the mercantile, she's disappointed. Caroline reminds Charles (who knows that Laura is bummed about the gift), "She's got to learn to be happy getting what she needs. Besides, years from now, when things like fancy mirrors are broken and long forgotten, she'll still be using that dictionary and thinking what a beautiful gift it was." ***This is a great reminder for our children, who are growing up in a world of instant gratification (and in many cases, extravagance).*** I frequently remind my children, who ask for an in-ground pool, fancy trips, a better phone, or a summer house at the beach (or all four!), that those things are wonderful but aren't necessarily the norm. ***It's important to remember that many people don't even have what they need, let alone anything luxurious. I think it's wise to teach our children to be grateful for what they have, as the Ingalls did.***

While Laura understands that her dictionary is a practical gift, she still wishes she'd received something a bit more exciting and fun. As she looks in the mercantile window the next day with her friend "Anna," Nellie comes along with a bunch of other girls and asks Laura and Anna if they want to join her "club." While upstairs, Nellie dictates that she will be president of the club but that Anna can't be in it, because she stutters. This crushes the poor little girl and makes Laura angry.

Knowing that Nellie doesn't appreciate anything she has, Laura steals Nellie's music box. *BIG MISTAKE.* Nellie catches her with it and threatens to tell Charles and Caroline unless Laura does everything she says. As a result, Nellie makes Laura kiss her butt and blow off Anna.

It isn't until Nellie deceives Anna into thinking she is finally welcomed into the group and then rejects her that Laura loses her cool. She basically tells Nellie where she can shove her club and her music box. *YES, Laura! Awesome to see a child stand up to a bully and be able to confidently walk away.*

At home, Laura has to come clean about what has happened. "I didn't wanna tell you, because I knew how disappointed you'd be in me. I thought I could find a way to make it right by myself . . . but I couldn't."

"The reason you couldn't was because you were too busy avoiding the only *real* way: telling the truth," Pa says. ***Encouraging honesty in our children is Parenting 101. Again, children who are welcome to be completely honest with their parents will feel more secure and will trust in the importance of the truth.***

I can remember myself having a childhood "friend" who I tended to obey, because she would make my life miserable if I didn't. As an adult, I look back and realize that I should have told this girl to shove it. Nobody should be able to make another person fearful like that. On the prairie, folks would comment on this behavior by saying, "That's the meanest thing I ever did see." When it comes to manipulative bullies, ***my*** *comments are a bit more "modern" and not as polite.*

*****

Similar messages are delivered in the episodes "The Election" (season three), "Harriet's Happenings" (season five), and "For the Love of Nancy" (season eight). Each of these shows portrays bullying in a different way, which is great, because there are so very many ways that bullying can happen.

"The Election" introduces us to "Elmer," a gentle boy who is a bit slow in the classroom but has a huge heart for people and animals. Two older boys pick on him constantly, making him eat worms and pushing him in the mud. When Miss Beadle holds an election for Class President, the bullies nominate Elmer as a joke. They proceed to tease him, but he responds with kindness. Upon hearing that his campaign promise is to work toward stopping big kids from picking on younger ones, the students see Elmer in a new light. He wins the election! ***The children have learned that "different" doesn't have to mean "worse." It can mean kinder and wiser. They've learned that the best leaders often have the biggest hearts.***

*****

"Harriet's Happenings" is about Harriet's pursuit to publish gossip in the town newspaper. Many citizens are hurt by things she writes, but no one more than "Eric Schiller," an excellent student whose parents speak primarily German. When Harriet is annoyed that Eric beats Nellie for a place in the township spelling bee, she prints a blurb in the newspaper saying that it will be hard for Eric to win, considering he was born to "illiterate" parents. Charles decides to teach her a lesson and awaken the townspeople to the pain this newspaper is causing. While presiding over the church service (Charles wears *many* hats in Walnut Grove), he asks Harriet to do the first reading. Believing it's because she is "Walnut Grove's outstanding citizen," she proudly struts to the alter. However, when Charles hands her Mr. Schiller's bible, she finds a surprise inside.

"I can't read this!" Harriet scoffs.

"Why? Are you illiterate?" Charles asks.

"Of course not! This is written in some sort of foreign gibberish!"

"That's not gibberish," Charles explains. "It's German."

Harriet is pissed. "Just because I can't read German doesn't make me illiterate."

"I agree, Mrs. Oleson," Charles answers, pointing out that the Schillers aren't illiterate either, just because they can't read English.

Harriet slams the bible down and returns to her seat.

Go Charles! Way to set her straight. ***Quite simply, bullies can clearly be addressed by getting a taste of their own medicine. It doesn't have to be cruel; just REAL.***

*****

"For the Love of Nancy" addresses how bullies sometimes use others for their own good.

Nancy takes advantage of "Elmer" (another Elmer! It must've been a popular name on the prairie!). He is a new, very overweight boy at school who develops an immediate crush on her. When she sees what a good student Elmer is and how enamored he is with her, Nancy asks him to do her homework and chores, fight her battles in the recess yard, and basically be at her beck and call. No matter how many times she treats him like crap, Elmer keeps coming back for more. He wants to be accepted, but with Nancy, there are only ulterior motives. She is, for certain, the new Nellie! Needless to say, Elmer is hurt when a misunderstanding causes Nancy to get upset with him and call him a "big, fat slob!" Even when Elmer loses twelve pounds, Nancy tells him, "So what? You'd have to lose a hundred before anyone would notice." *Cringe.*

It's fabulous when the other children convince Elmer that he deserves better, and he finally tells Nancy where to go. Jogging past her as she tries to lure him to her rescue in a baseball game, Elmer says, "Sorry, Nancy. You're gonna have to work things out for yourself from now on." *Outstanding!* ***Sometimes all our kids need is to gain the confidence to politely shut down a bully. If we give them that confidence and they surround themselves with good people, they should be just fine!***

"There are a lot of things in this world that are more important than being popular. Being true to yourself is one of them."
—Michael Landon

Chapter 5
Discipline

*"If God Had Never Wanted Us to Say 'No' to Our Children,
He Would Never Have Invented the Word!"*

AH, DISCIPLINE. A PARENT'S FAVORITE WORD (or not). "Discipline" may have only one or two definitions in the dictionary, but this word has more meanings than most. After all, ***discipline takes a different form in every household. Parents have their own individual ideas about how to run the house, and each child responds in his or her own way to various rules and punishments.*** For example, when I was young, all my mom had to do was threaten to send me to my room. I *hated* being sent to my room. My brother, on the other hand, if sent to his room, would read a book or listen to music very happily. As a result, my parents had to come up with different consequences for the two of us. Discipline goes far beyond punishments for "bad" behavior. In my experience, it's a practice that seems to last from every sunrise to every sunset as we're raising our kids; teaching manners, instilling responsibility, discouraging backtalk . . . As I write this, the scent of microwave popcorn is wafting into my office from the kitchen. It's lunchtime in the summer. My son has gotten into the habit of eating an entire bag of popcorn as his midday meal. As many times as I've said, "Make yourself a sandwich and have a little popcorn on the side," he isn't listening. In fact, I had stopped buying popcorn altogether for just this reason. This is the first box we've had in a while. Won't be buying it again! That'll "learn him!"

Little House on the Prairie gives lots of ideas for disciplining our children. I have to say, first and foremost in this chapter: If you want to see what to do with regard to disciplining your children, watch how *Laura and Almanzo* deal with Myron and Rupert in the episode "The Nephews" (season seven). If you want to see what *not* to do with regard to disciplining your children, watch how "*Royal and Millie*" deal with Myron and Rupert in the episode "The Nephews." I'll just leave that little tidbit right there (Pssst .... Royal and Millie don't believe in saying "No." Good God, save us all!).

Discipline. Charles and Caroline approach this piece of their family life in remarkable ways. One scene that comes to mind is from the episode "The Award" (season one). While Charles is away on a trip, Mary becomes obsessed with the possibility of winning a beautiful book at school by achieving the highest score on a special examination. Finding that she doesn't have enough hours in the day to read all that she wants to, she decides to go to the barn in the middle of the night to study. The problem? She has to light a lantern, and barns are full of hay *(key up the "impending doom" music).* Mary falls asleep and kicks the lantern over, setting the barn on fire.

"HOW MANY TIMES HAVE I TOLD YOU NEVER TO LIGHT MATCHES OR LANTERNS IN THE BARN?!!" Caroline yells after she manages to put the fire out. "BUT YOU FORGOT?!! Well, Young Lady, you're gonna remember from this night on! And you can forget that examination! Tomorrow I want you to go in and tell Miss Beadle that you're not taking it! Now go on to bed!"

Like any of us probably would, Ma has lost her shit. However, the next day, when she's feeling calmer, she explains to Mary that she was so harsh the night before because she was very frightened. Fair enough. She also goes to town to see "Reverend Alden."

"I lost my temper," Caroline tells him, "and I *never* lose my temper with my girls."

How many of us moms can say THAT??? (Cricket, cricket . . .)

Reverend Alden smiles. "There are few among us who haven't said or done something we regret. Did Mary say she was sorry?"

"Oh, several times," Caroline continues.

Reverend Alden grins. "Doesn't that say quite a lot? She's accepted the responsibility and she's trying to make amends. A few days, and she is going to be the Mary you always knew."

"But what about the examination?" Caroline is torn.

The reverend levels with her. "If you forget this punishment, all your girls could expect you to forget the next one, and the next one after that . . . Family discipline is based on promises kept, for punishment or reward. Without constancy, a child has no rules to live by."

"Nor do we," Caroline agrees.

A perfect conversation. The reverend helps Caroline realize that, in losing her cool, she's only human. He also emphasizes the importance of consistency and follow-through.

These two things are, in my opinion, the key factors in disciplining our kids. Establishing solid rules and expectations in our homes gives our children a sense of safety. And then, when we enforce those rules, it creates a truth about the family they know they can count on.

I try to choose my words very carefully with my kids, especially when threatening a consequence. It's counterproductive to make threats if we don't follow through with them, because we will lose all credibility with our children. Then they'll *never* listen to us!

Like Mary did in "The Award," ***our children need to learn a sense of responsibility, and they have to be held accountable for their actions.***

*****

In "The Castoffs" (season four), Laura is itching to go into town and visit a new neighbor who has moved to Walnut Grove. However, Caroline insists that she first take the foxtails out of her dog's ears. Laura is not psyched. She tries to negotiate with Ma, but Caroline won't have it.

"Laura, Jack is *your* dog! You've been neglecting him." Before she's allowed to do anything else, Laura has to take care of Jack. Plain and simple.

*****

In an episode called "The Gift" (season two), Laura and Mary are entrusted with the Sunday School fund, with which they have been instructed to buy a new bible for Reverend Alden. Laura talks Mary into ordering a case of medicine instead. She figures they will sell all of the bottles and make enough money to buy the best, most expensive bible. When no one wants to buy the medicine, the girls know they've messed up. Now they have no money *and* no bible.

On the day they're supposed to present the gift to Revered Alden, Mary and Laura both pretend to be sick in bed.

"We just *can't* go to church, Pa," Mary groans.

"We have Leren-GHEE-us," Laura mumbles.

"You have *what*?" Charles asks.

"La-RANG-it-is," Mary corrects her.

Charles knows something's up. He plays along. "How long do you think this 'La-RANG-it-is' is gonna last?"

"We need a few more hours to get over it, Pa," Laura says.

"You mean by the time Ma and Carrie and I get back from church, you'll be feeling better then?"

Mary nods. "We just have to get our strength back."

"Yeah." Charles says sternly. "First of all, it's pronounced *laryngitis*, and it means you can't talk."

GULP.

Charles asks for an explanation, and this time, the girls tell him the truth. They beg him not to be mad and to let them stay home. *No deal.*

"I think you two better get dressed. I don't want you to be late for church."

"But, Pa-"

"No buts about it. Now, you made a mistake; you've gotta own up to it. I'll be waiting for you downstairs. I know this won't be easy for you, but you can't hide what you did forever. Now c'mon. Get ready."

Good dad, great lesson! Charles doesn't pardon what his girls did, make excuses for them, or talk to Reverend Alden for them. They have to assume all of the responsibility on their own.

The way we address our children when we aren't happy with something they've done can be helpful or harmful. Charles and Caroline always seem to know just the right way to approach things.

*****

In the beginning of season five, the Ingalls move to the city. There, the kids are exposed to much more "colorful" language and behavior than they're used to seeing in Walnut Grove. At the dinner table one night, Carrie's food falls off her fork.

"Oh, DAMN!" she exclaims.

Every head snaps around.

"Don't ever let me hear you talk like that!" Caroline scolds.

Laura explains that they hear talk like this coming from the saloon all night long. Charles advises Carrie to come to him or Caroline the next time she hears a word she doesn't understand.

"She can ask me," Laura suggests.

Charles glares at her. "Why, do you know all the bad words?"

OOPS.

"No, Sir."

"Well it's lucky for you that you don't. Now eat your supper."

This whole exchange is handled quietly and calmly. ***The kids know their parents aren't happy, but no explosion has taken place. Just a conversation. Nice. I often find it difficult to stay as calm, cool, and collected as Charles and Caroline do. Oh, Damn. I guess it takes practice.***

*****

Similar examples are presented in the episode "The Handyman" (season four). Charles is (again) away for work, and Caroline has hired a handyman to complete the kitchen addition that Charles started before he was called away. Not surprisingly, the very handsome guy (named "Chris") falls for beautiful Caroline during his time at the house. He is also "smitten" in a fatherly way with Mary, Laura, and Carrie, who call him "Uncle Chris" and enjoy having him around. However, once Mary realizes that he has feelings for her mother, she becomes very mistrusting and angry. When the girls arrive home from school one day and see Chris wearing one of their pa's shirts, Mary confronts Caroline.

"I wanna know why *he's* wearing the shirt I made for Pa!" Mary demands forcefully.

Caroline answers very calmly, "Because he fell and tore his, and got blood on it. Now suppose you tell me why you're using that tone of voice." ***Gentle but firm. So simple!*** My typical response when my children raise their voice to me is (raising my voice right back), "Who do you think you're talking to?!?!" *Ugh. More practice needed over here.*

Mary realizes that she's overreacted. "I'm sorry."

"Apology accepted," Caroline says. "Now what happened today to put you in this mood? . . . Ya know, you're gonna have to learn how to control your temper," Caroline smiles.

I guess sometimes we can get to the bottom of our children's bad moods and fresh tones by just talking things out. We just have to hope that they respond

as reasonably! Quite often their reactions to upsetting situations are either escalated or calmed by how WE react.

Listening can be a very integral part of disciplining, too.

*****

Caroline's calm nature, even while disciplining her child, is again shown to us in the (sad and disturbing) episode "Sylvia" (season seven). This one scared the crap out of me as a kid! It was so "un-*Little House*" that I've always wondered where it came from. I'm guessing they were trying to either touch on very serious topics or boost ratings (or both). A girl named Sylvia has "developed" more than the other girls in the school, and the boys all enjoy looking at her. A grown man is also watching her – from afar – and one day, as she's walking home through the woods, he grabs her from behind. He's wearing a creepy clown mask and pulls her down to the ground. Thank goodness we don't see any more of this violent act, but we know he rapes her. *Awful. To this day, I'm still afraid to walk in the woods by myself, and I'm still unable to watch the scene where that black glove covers Sylvia's mouth and that clown mask appears. I can't look at the scene where he finds her again at the end, either. Totally terrifying. I* ***much*** *prefer the lighthearted times on the prairie!*

When Mrs. Oleson finds out that Sylvia is pregnant, she spreads a lie in town that Albert is the father. *Wretch!*

Albert decides he should marry Sylvia, so that he can take care of her and the baby. The scene when he springs this news on Charles and Caroline is bone-chilling. The looks exchanged between them are intense, and the silence is deafening (except of course, for the thunderstorm that is *always* happening during a scene like this).

Charles is shocked and appalled, becoming angry almost immediately.

"Look Albert, I know you care for this girl, I know you feel sorry for her, but you can't marry someone because you feel sorry for them."

"I wanna marry her because I *love* her!" Albert clarifies firmly. "The baby's not mine, but it's part of her. Of someone I love!"

"It's not the same," Charles says.

"Then you lied to me, Pa. I'm not your son either, but you told me you love me just the same. Were you lyin'?"

Whoa. Charles has been schooled. He leaves the room, saying to Caroline on his way out, "Just try and talk some sense into him."

This scene is, in my opinion, one of Karen Grassle's best ever. She is just brilliant here. Caroline wipes the tears from her eyes and gently speaks to her son. "Albert . . . A boy your age has no idea-"

Albert cuts her off. "Ma, please don't tell me I'm too young to know *how **I feel!***" His voice becomes increasingly louder.

Caroline understands that he's upset, but she's not having this tone from Albert at all. "I wasn't going to try and tell you that. And don't ever raise your voice to me while you live in this house!" Now *her* tone is curt and cutting. *I've always loved this simple line, which says a **whole lot** about how we will or will not allow our children to speak to us.*

Albert is taken aback.

Caroline asks him how Sylvia feels about the baby. "That child wasn't conceived in love. It was a cruel, a brutal thing. It won't be that easy for that girl to forget. How will she feel about that child?"

Caroline has struck a nerve. Albert breaks down in tears and hugs her. "I don't know, Ma. I just know I love her."

"I know. I know." Caroline holds her son. ***Again, she has made her child feel heard and understood while also managing to help him see another side of things. She has expressed disagreement with Albert's plans without projecting disapproval of him. She's allowed her son to express his frustration without allowing him to be disrespectful of her. Cutting Albert's attitude right off when he raises his voice to her is perfect. Caroline listens calmly, which keeps the whole interaction calm. When we listen to our children without being judgmental about what we're hearing, they may open up to us more readily.***

"I want people to laugh and cry, not just sit there and stare at the TV."
—Michael Landon

Chapter 6
Listening to Our Children

"It Took the Children of This Town to Show Us . . ."

While we're on the subject of listening, why not devote a chapter to it? Children, who have learned to walk, talk, and learn a foreign language all since their birth, are pretty brilliant, wouldn't you say? Quite often, their straight-forward, logical thinking is worth hearing. As most of us have found, our children frequently teach us as much as we teach them (or more).

The people of Walnut Grove find this to be true in the episode "The Voice of Tinker Jones" (season one). Reverend Alden expresses interest in getting a church bell to call the congregation to services on Sunday mornings. Harriet offers to donate the bell (along with a plaque saying she did so, of course!). While some of the townspeople wish to accept Harriet's gift, other church members feel that a community donation should be collected so that the bell and church aren't dedicated to one person/family. A town argument ensues, affecting both adults and children.

The kids are distraught over their parents' quarreling. They aren't alone. "Tinker Jones," a mute silversmith, is saddened that his community is being torn apart. He decides to enlist the children to help him make a bell for the church and school to use. They keep it a secret until it's finished. Then, one Sunday morning, the ringing of the bell awakens everyone for miles around. Members of the congregation get dressed and hurry into town. Immediately, people begin to accuse each other of purchasing the bell behind the others' backs.

"It was Tinker Jones' idea," Mary tells everyone.

"*Tinker* made the bell," Willie says.

"He did it so we would all stop fighting and become friends," Laura explains.

"And have church here . . . like we used to," adds Mary.

The parents look ashamed and happy at the same time. Tinker signs to the crowd that the kids all helped him make the bell. ***The children beam with pride. They have taught their parents a lesson: to put differences aside for the sake of the group. Better than that, the children have been heard. Listening to our children's concerns and looking at things through their eyes from time to time isn't such a bad idea.***

*****

"Peter," the main character in the episode "The Stranger" (season four), does *not* feel heard by his father. Son to an important, wealthy businessman, Peter attends a private boarding school but is expelled for cheating and stealing.

"We'll discuss it later," his father tells him. Peter can't believe it. How can his own father not care that he's been kicked out of school? Banished to his room, Peter is hurt and angry. When "later" comes, his father's solution is to send him away to stay with Nels (his cousin) and Harriet in Walnut Grove, where Peter can learn a sense of values.

Peter feels unloved, as though he's being cast off so that his father doesn't have to deal with him. This is probably the worst kind of rejection a child can feel. Peter causes all kinds of trouble at the Olesons' house, to the point where Nels and Harriet can't handle him.

Charles to the rescue! He explains to Nels that he could use some help around the farm and would be happy to hire Peter, allowing him to stay with the Ingalls for a while. This is where the boy is *really* introduced to the values of prairie life! As he learns to "chop two wagonloads," milk a cow (squirting Laura in the eye), and drive a team, Peter comes to love the Ingalls family, even calling Pa "Uncle Charles."

The most exciting thing for Peter is learning to swim. He is so proud, but when his father and grandmother come to take him home, Peter is crushed when he tries to show them how he can swim, and his father doesn't even notice.

"I'm sure there are a lot of things you don't know about your son," Charles says. "Are you aware that he doesn't like school, that he steals things . . . so that you'll pay attention to him? So that at least you'll *have* to talk to him? . . . There's a lot more to raising a boy than teaching him a sense of values. There is *love*, Sir."

This exchange could bring *anyone* to tears. ***Listening to our children gives us a glimpse into what they're feeling and experiencing as members of our family. There aren't too many things more important than our children's feelings. Our kids need us to hear them, about their thoughts, fears, hopes, education, race, religion, questions, dreams . . . They need us to listen. I once saw a very powerful quote posted on Facebook by a friend of mine which said, "We love the children God has given us, not the children we wish they would be." I LOVE this. All we need to do is listen and allow our kids to be their true selves.***

*****

"Fight Team, Fight!" (season seven) centers around the game of football, but it touches more importantly on listening to our children's concerns about their activities. As a "sports mom," I have seen all too often the tendency of parents to place unbelievable pressure on their kids when it comes to athletics. I've also noticed the extreme emphasis placed on winning. I "had words" one afternoon with a disgruntled mother at the baseball field before my son's game. We arrived at the field early and watched the end of the previous game. We were standing near the parents of the team that lost.

"Good luck to *you* guys if you get *this* ump! He sucks!" one of the moms yelled to us.

"You're terrible, Ump!" screamed another.

The umpire, who looked like he was about seventeen years old, didn't respond.

One of the dads from our team said to the women, "Take it easy! He's just a kid."

The women did *not* appreciate this at all.

"So are *they*!" one of them yelled, pointing to her son's team. "*Our* kids are only ten!"

I calmly but firmly answered, "All the more reason for you to stop screaming in front of them. *And* in front of *our* kids." I was very proud of my Caroline-esque way of addressing this lunatic. Over-the-top sports parents really put a bee in my bonnet.

In my opinion, our children's sports are meant for fun and social interaction. Being that I've never been an overly competitive person, ***I see these activities as opportunities for our kids to practice doing their best and to learn sportsmanship, essential game skills, and camaraderie. We have a rule during our car ride home after a game: no discussing the game, except for compliments. If our child wants to talk about specifics, we absolutely will listen and join in, but we try to keep it positive.***

In "Fight, Team, Fight!" college football star "Pete Elerbee" returns to Walnut Grove and takes over as coach of the kinda-sucky football team. His son, "Dan," is a mediocre player who is okay with the game but plays mostly to earn his father's approval. The show opens with Dan showing his parents his artwork during dinner.

"Pete," Dan's mother says, passing the drawing to her husband, "our son has quite a talent!"

"Too bad it doesn't extend to football," Pete says, blowing off his son's art.

Ouch. It's unfortunate that Dan's mother is the only one who "listens" to

Dan's silent pleas to be freed from this sport he despises and to be able to pursue his own interests.

Pete is determined to turn Walnut Grove's boys into a championship football team and works them until they can barely stand. He is extra hard on Dan, who looks miserable.

One night, after losing a big game, Dan opens up to his mother. "I don't wanna play anymore. I never wanted to play in the first place . . . I did my best today. I did. I can't be what he wants me to be. I want him to love me, but . . . " Tears fall.

Pete's wife tells him that when he lost that game, he also lost his son; that Dan doesn't need a coach, he needs a father to hold him and love him; that knowing how to love people is what makes someone a man.

The next day, Albert has some words of wisdom for Pete as well. "I don't mean to say that I didn't appreciate playing . . . all of the things you taught me about team spirit, needing to win, not giving up . . . But ya see, Sir, I plan to grow up to be a doctor, not a football player. It's just a game to me; and games are fun. Football *used* to be fun. Maybe we lost all but one game last year, but it was still fun! Mr. Elerbee, playing this way just isn't fun. Good luck with the team."

Pete decides to go talk to his son. He has a lot of wrongs to right. *Hallelujah!* ***Our children need our ears. They need us to be insightful. They need us to accept them as they are.***

If we listen, they'll show us who they are. All we need to do is hear our kids and allow them to be their true selves.

I believe in God, family, truth between people, the power of love.
—Michael Landon

Chapter 7
Schooling

"Ma? How Long's All This Learning Gonna Take?"

Remember Walnut Grove's one-room schoolhouse? As small as it was, I think it must've been really challenging for a teacher on the prairie to teach one class when the students were of all different ages and levels. "Landsakes!" This could transform "No Child Left Behind" into "No Teacher Left Standing!" When I was teaching elementary school, I always found it interesting that when I met people and they asked what I did for living, my response was rarely followed by any further questions. Everyone pretty much "knows" about teachers, because everyone went to school. Right? Nope. Like any other job, it is hard work, and no one really knows what a teacher's day is like unless they live it. Teaching is one of those jobs that involves endless work and endless love.

Between Miss Beadle, Mrs. Garvey, Miss Wilder, Laura, and Miss Plum (plus a few strays thrown in along the way), the Walnut Grove teachers sure see *a lot* in that one little room over the years.

Before Laura and Mary leave for school on their very first day, Caroline says, "We start learning when we're born. And if we're wise, we don't stop until the Lord calls us home."

Both students *and* teachers are nervous on the first day of school. Mary and Laura have some extra anxiety, being new in town. It doesn't help when the other kids look at their short dresses and chant, "Snipes! Snipes! Long-legged snipes!" Laura is laughed at for not knowing how Willie's chalk writing can be cleared from the blackboard.

Miss Beadle, always sensitive and diplomatic, says, "Willie, Laura has asked a question. Will you please demonstrate the answer?" *Nicely handled.*

Also awesome in this episode is the way Miss Beadle works with Laura; patient and thorough as Laura learns how to read. When the entire class is instructed to write essays for "Parents' Day," Laura stands up in front of everyone and delivers the sweetest, most loving tribute to her mother. Later, Miss Beadle says to her, "You gave one of the finest recitations it's been my pleasure to hear."

Knowing that Laura is not at all capable yet of writing what she actually said that day, Caroline wants Laura to show Miss Beadle her paper. It only says:

Ma is good.

She works hard.

She cooks.

She sews.

Neither Laura nor Caroline know how Miss Beadle will react. But the amazing teacher pleasantly nods and smiles. "Laura's spelling has improved a great deal. Her penmanship needs a little improvement . . . But I think with a lot of hard work, by the time school's out, she'll have that mastered as well."

One gift of a fine teacher is knowing how to make compliments abundant while gently pointing out what skills need more attention. We can use this approach in our parenting, too. After all, according to Caroline, "a mother is all things: a cook, a dressmaker, a disciplinarian, a nurse . . . But above all, a teacher." As parents, we teach our children every day, and our lessons shape them. Doing so in a positive way will give our children confidence. Our compliments can be abundant, while criticisms can be present but more subtle, just like Miss Beadle's perfectly-balanced approach to Laura's essay.

*****

Caroline is given the chance to find this balance when she is asked to teach temporarily in the episode "School Mom" (season one). I admire her spunk and courage in this story. When she's challenged by one of the kids about her teaching qualifications, Caroline says, "It's not easy to know what someone else can do until you give him or her a chance. Tell me, Harry, what do you do best?"

"I can bat a ball farther than most anyone. Most men even!" Harry boasts.

"Well, all right," Caroline says. "Suppose you show us?" She instructs all the kids to come outside.

Harry hits the ball hard. Then he hands the bat to Caroline. "Your turn."

DOH!

Caroline nervously steps up to the plate and raises the bat. In comes the pitch, and SMACK! She wails it out of the schoolyard, even shocking herself.

When she later calls on an older boy named "Abel" to read aloud, he stands up but fumbles to speak. The children begin to giggle. What Caroline doesn't know is that Abel can't read and has always had trouble in school. He becomes humiliated and walks out.

Caroline knows at that moment that she has to help this boy. She admires and compliments the pottery work he's done at home, making him feel proud. The two work together until Abel can read and spell. There's no greater sense of accomplishment as a teacher or a parent than knowing you have helped a child feel successful. ***When our children struggle, whether it be with academics, social situations, sports, or anything else, it is our compassion and understanding that can help see them through. Our time, our encouragement, and a push to work hard are key ingredients in helping them rise above adversity.***

On Caroline's last day of teaching, Abel reads a note on behalf of all the students. "We want to thank you, Mrs. Ingalls. You are a fine teacher and a good friend to us all." Caroline is so moved, not only by what the note says, but by the fact that Abel can now read because of her love and persistence. All the kids love her. They respect her, because she is a good, kind, fair teacher. ***As***

parents, we know our kids love us; but we can be sure that they will respect us more if we are firm but fair, structured yet loving.

We all remember our favorite teacher(s). Whenever I tell someone that I used to teach third grade, (s)he either says, "I *loved* my third grade teacher," or "I *hated* my third grade teacher." It's pretty funny. Even though we're still so young during our elementary years, those teachers have quite an impact on us. My second grade teacher recognized my love for writing and bought me my very own notebook in which to write my stories and poems. This made me feel so special and actually prompted my decision (at age 8) to become an author. My third grader teacher further encouraged my writing, making my choice even more solid. To this day – forty years later – I'm so grateful for those two teachers! One of my best days to date was when I was invited by the elementary school I attended to return as a visiting children's author. The greatest part? My second grade teacher was there!

*****

Children will go to great lengths to respect and protect a teacher they love. Miss Beadle finds this in the episode "Troublemaker" (season two). Not at first, however. The older boys are being extremely disruptive with their pranks and loud noises all day in class. One afternoon, a fight breaks out during a lesson. Unfortunately, it happens just as Harriet (her timing is always unreal) and town councilman "Mr. Hanson" walk in.

A school board meeting that night results in the hiring of a male replacement for Miss Beadle. "Mr. Applewood," an extremely stern, middle-aged fellow, is a nightmare from the start. The kids quickly give him the nickname "Crabapple." He is very strict with the entire class, but he's got it IN for Laura.

Seeing her as the former teacher's pet and a troublemaker, Mr. Applewood punishes Laura repeatedly in class and eventually expels her for something she didn't even do. When Charles calls him out, Mr. Applewood makes the *(BIG!)* mistake of grabbing him. *NOT A WISE IDEA, Crabapple! Don't you know who you're messin' with???* Charles grabs him right back, pushing him up against the school building.

At the next board meeting, the shit hits the (nonexistent, pre-electricity) fan. Mr. Applewood flies into a rage, ranting and raving about how he needs routine, rules, and order. "I MUST HAVE ORDER!" he demands, slamming his fist on the desk, his entire body shaking. Now everyone in the room knows he's a looney control freak.

The interesting thing in this schoolhouse story is that Crabapple's evil demeanor has turned all of his students against him. As a result, anything negative that happens to him is perceived by the kids as funny. They aren't interested in respecting him, because they aren't getting any respect from him. Children will do this with their parents as well. Sometimes (especially during the teenage years), the power struggle is as real as the day is long! Asking ourselves, "Who is the adult here?" can help keep us in check. We have to give respect in order to get it from our kids in return.

*****

Encouraging our children to work hard is a natural parenting move. Just as important is assuring them that their best effort is enough. Caroline does a great job of this in an episode called "The Pride of Walnut Grove" (season two). Mary is thrilled when she is chosen to participate in a statewide mathematics competition. She is representing her area of Minnesota, so she feels pressured to do well. I really love how Caroline speaks to Mary throughout this episode. During her lunch break on the day of the exam, Mary says to Caroline, "I've never seen such problems! There was this one about a train. I didn't think I'd ever get it!"

Always positive, Caroline tells her, "Well, at least that problem's over. You don't have to think about it anymore."

"I just don't think I'm doing well, Ma," Mary frowns.

"Are you doing your best?" Caroline asks.

"Yes," says Mary quietly.

Caroline smiles. "Then that's all you can do!"

I LOVE her!

"Just do your best." This very simple idea can be so empowering for kids (and adults too!).

"For me, I want to tell stories that will affect my children in a positive way, that they can be proud of me for working on and doing. I want to be a light in the world. There's enough darkness."

—Michael Landon

Chapter 8
Working Hard for What We Want

"Somebody Once Said, 'There's No Reason to Be Ashamed of Any Job, as Long as You Do Your Best.' "

One very significant, recurring theme in *Little House* is the importance of working hard. Aside from the fact that life on the prairie is challenging to begin with, the Ingalls are dealing with poverty as well. As a result, Charles and Caroline (and oftentimes their children) make great sacrifices on a fairly regular basis, and working hard is just part of their "normal."

"The 100 Mile Walk" is episode three of the entire series, and it dives right into the hardships faced by farming families. After they grow a beautiful wheat crop, a hail storm destroys it, and all the Ingalls' plans are destroyed with it. Charles has to go away to look for work and sets out on foot. On the road, he meets up with "Jack" and "Jacob," both of whom are also looking for work. Jack is a spirited, happy-go-lucky type. He describes railroad double-jack work to Charles and Jacob. It involves drilling holes in boulders so that dynamite can be inserted. Jack is able to recommend them for the job, and they get it.

Side note: At the gym where I work out, my coach has our group do "Sledgehammers" as one of our exercises. We literally use sledgehammers and swing them up, around over our heads, and slam them onto a huge tire on the floor. The first time I saw the exercise demonstrated, I chuckled to myself. Then I picked up that sledgehammer and, with nearly perfect form, I swung that thing around like a pro. Winking at my friend, Caroline, I giggled, "Ya know why I'm so good at this? Because I learned from the best; Charles Ingalls on Little House." Now I love whenever sledgehammers are part of our workouts. If this author gig doesn't work out, maybe I'll become a double-jacker.

When I was a kid, I cracked up watching the scene where Charles and Jacob observe a double-jack team. Jack explains, "The man with the double-jack, all he needs is a good eye. The man holding the drill? A strong nose."

"What if the hammer misses?" Jacob asks nervously.

"If the hammer misses?" Jack giggles. "The man holding the drill will have to pick his nose with his elbow."

Charles wiggles his nose apprehensively.

Meanwhile, Caroline holds a meeting at her house for the women in town. She talks to them about working together to save the wheat that has been harmed by the storm. Not afraid of hard work, the women decide to go for it. All the children help, too. *Hmmm . . . Kids harvesting a crop? Quite different from the McDonalds drive thru, huh?*

Charles' job goes well, and the women are successful in harvesting the wheat. The family knows there'll be enough money and food to make it through the winter, all because they have worked hard and never questioned that commitment to their family. Even though they are one hundred miles apart, ***they work together and do what they have to do to support their family and keep everyone together.***

Meanwhile, in my house, it's like pulling teeth to get my kids to pick up their shoes! Sheesh. It's important to me that they have certain chores around the house. They need that sense of responsibility. I also think it's healthy for them to know the significance of helping others and working together to accomplish something. Trying to get them involved in the community is another goal I keep. We live in a world where so much is done for us. I don't want my kids to be afraid to get their hands dirty and really work hard for what they want. As a writer, I work from home. To my kids, this means I don't work. Heavy sigh. I guess they don't consider cooking, doing laundry, cleaning, and playing referee to be actual work. They also don't count the hours I sit at my computer, tapping away on the keys, working on my next book . . . Believe it or not, there's something to be said for the pile of rejection letters I have accumulated from publishers. It takes determination to build that kind of "rejection collection!" Seriously, though, I like my kids to see me at my desk, working hard to achieve my goals. I am truly "living the dream."

Laboring for what we want in life gives us an immediate sense of commitment and an eventual sense of accomplishment. Practicing this with my kids is something I'm always working on. Especially during this really strange, isolating time of quarantine, it's really easy to feel badly for my kids. They're missing out on a lot; we all are. So it's tempting to try to keep them happy by giving them things, providing comfort food, and making special purchases. I guess this is fine, but I also want to use this time to teach them to work more for what they **want**. ***You wanna buy that Fortnite skin? Sure, after you clean the bathroom. You'd like to have ice cream tonight? No problem! Pick up your room and put your clothes away. Can you have extra screen time? Maybe, after you walk the dog.***

*****

It's kind of funny how, on the prairie, the kids were expected to do all kinds of chores in addition to their schoolwork, but when it came to women working outside the house, that was often a big no-no. Okay, so, basically a girl went to school for all those years while also learning responsible skills around the home and farm. Then, when she graduated and got married, she was told she shouldn't get a job. Obviously, I realize that it was a different time; it's just fascinating compared to the mindset in our country today.

Several episodes of *Little House* show us male opposition to a female working outside the home. "The High Cost of Being Right" (season four) is about the Garvey family. In this episode, they are extremely happy and grateful that their crop has done so well. Unfortunately, all they have harvested is stored in the barn, which burns down unexpectedly. They are left with nothing. Jonathan is so angry that he lashes out at family and friends.

After a few days, Alice finds work in town.

"Ya ain't takin' no job," Jonathan says flatly. As hard as Alice tries to convince him that the job will help the family, Jonathan stubbornly refuses to agree.

C'mon, Dude. Your woman is trying to save your ass. Buck up and accept!

Unable to see eye to eye about their situation, Alice and Jonathan decide to separate. When a circuit judge arrives to handle the divorce, Charles and Caroline act as witnesses. This scene is *hilarious*! "Judge Picker" is played by Eddie Quillan (who actually appears in several *Little House* episodes over the years). His voice and facial expressions are hysterical!

"I will assume that, as usual, there are questions of property and other financial matters which are not yet settled between you. I will state categorically that unless they are settled here and now, in my presence, and to the satisfaction of all parties, you will need to engage in separate attorneys and go fight it out in Minneapolis. That's a very expensive proposition, so I suggest you consider it when either or both of you are tempted to succumb to unreasonableness."

"You don't have to worry about that, Your Honor," Jonathan says. "We ain't unreasonable people."

Judge Picker looks puzzled. "Somebody must be. You're getting divorced!"

"Your Honor," Alice says, "I can promise you, there's no problem concerning money or property. I'll go along with whatever my husband thinks is fair."

"Most unusual," the judge comments, scratching his beard. "Is there anything that is not resolved between you?"

Alice says, "Yes. One thing. The custody of our son. Jonathan, he wants to live with you. I've agreed," Alice tells him, "so long as you remain in Walnut Grove."

Andy says, "It'll be the next best thing to still being a family. Even if you hate each other, it doesn't mean I still don't love both of you."

Sniffle, sniffle.

"I don't hate your ma, Boy," says Jonathan.

"Then why are you getting a divorce?" Andy asks.

"Ask your mother."

Wimpy response!

"Why, Ma?" Andy wants to know. Alice doesn't know what to say.

"Tell him it's because I'm a failure," Jonathan starts in. "I'm useless. If a man can't provide for his family, he got no right to be a husband."

"I never said that," Alice disagrees. I never even hinted that I see you that way."

"Ya did too."

"When?"

"Lots of times."

"*When*?!?!"

"You tellin' me I didn't hear those accusing things you said to me?"

"No, I'm not. I believe you heard them; I just never *said* them. Sometimes I think you block out my voice and put in a voice from your own head!"

"Oh, that's really great. Now you're telling me I'm crazy!" Jonathan says.

"There, ya see? I *never* said you were crazy! You just said I said you were crazy!"

"I didn't."

"You did too!" Alice argues back.

"I said *you* said!"

"I *said* that you never hear what I say!"

"Well, I'm hearin' ya now."

"Then what did I say?"

"You said I was crazy!"

Suddenly, Charles bursts out laughing from the back of the room. Caroline tries to shush him. *Michael Landon's laugh here … Oh my gosh! Hilarious!*

Jonathan looks annoyed. "Charles, I don't see nothin' funny."

"I'm sorry!" Charles laughs.

"You better tell me why you're laughin.' "

Charles can barely form words. "He says that she says . . . *She* didn't say you were crazy. *YOU* said you were crazy!"

"Well, what *did* she say?" Jonathan asks.

"*I* don't know what she said!" Charles continues to laugh hysterically.

"What *did* you say?" Jonathan asks Alice.

Caroline starts to laugh too. Then Alice. Then Jonathan. Then Andy. Jonathan and Alice hug, as everyone continues to crack up.

Judge Picker is baffled. "I would just like to know, are we or are we not getting a divorce?"

Jonathan continues to hug his wife and answers, "Well, I don't know . . . *Are* you?"

Everyone explodes again. Judge Picker tells them they're ALL crazy.

This is a fun scene that places a happy ending on a tense situation; and it all started with a man's opposition to his woman getting a job. ***I love how this episode reminds us to check ourselves. Am I being reasonable? Am I really listening to the other person? Have I misinterpreted what (s)he said because of my own self-doubt?*** Jonathan is fixated on his debt rather than seeing Alice's job as a way *out* of that debt. She doesn't see it as supporting him financially, but rather a way to help their family during a tough time. ***I also think that this ending points out the importance of being able to laugh at ourselves and at some of life's situations. Having a sense of humor can really be helpful during trying periods in our lives.***

Fun fact: Hersha Parady, who played Alice, loved this episode but hated the ending. "All that laughing was just silly!" she told me. Hersha felt that the problems between Jonathan and Alice weren't really resolved this way; but she really enjoyed having a storyline about her character. I loved her in this episode!

*****

By the seventh season, Laura and Almanzo have fallen in love and are engaged to be married. Laura is honored when she finds out that she's been chosen for a teaching position in another town.

Almanzo isn't quite as thrilled when he hears the news. "I don't understand. I just don't know why you applied … Don't you think I can provide for us?" *"Manly" is a bit snippy here.*

"Of course I do. My ma works, ya know."

"I know," Almanzo says. "That may be all right with your pa, but it's not all right with me. Ya understand?" *Remember the "nincompoop" we mentioned earlier? Mmm-hmmmm.*

When the man who has sold Almanzo a piece of property also sells him out by damming up the stream leading to the land, Almanzo knows that his new land won't be farmable. He postpones the wedding, telling Laura, "I can't marry you now. I just lost the farm; I can't put a roof over your head . . . I just can't get married until I can provide."

Laura finds out that the teaching position is still available, and she is once again thrilled. Almanzo? Once again *not* thrilled.

"No. No. I don't want you to take the job. I don't need your money to build us a house or buy us a farm." *Stubborn.* Pigheaded Manly refuses to change his mind, and Laura continues to stand her ground. It takes her leaving town for Almanzo to realize that her work is a valuable asset in their lives at this moment.

It's encouraging to see in these various episodes how the women can (eventually) convince their men that a female working doesn't make a male look any less strong or important. Families work together emotionally, physically, and financially. I'm really glad that in today's society, anything goes. It's acceptable for both parents to work. It's acceptable for the wife to work while the husband cares for the children. It's acceptable for the wife to stay home with the children while the man works. I feel very fortunate that I've been able to stay home and raise my children while also working on my writing. Some women have told me they would be too bored staying home. I can respect that. Every family has to do whatever works best for them. I appreciate this model more than the traditional prairie model. Glad times have changed!

*****

Albert is the main character in the episode "The Craftsman" (season five). He takes a job as an apprentice to a coffin maker. He's interested in learning a trade and is intrigued by the work of Mr. Singerman. The old man teaches Albert lessons in both woodworking and life.

As they're making a coffin one day, Albert says to Mr. Singerman, "This sure would've been a lot easier to make if we used nails."

Mr. Singerman disagrees. "Never. Nails are an abomination to a true craftsman."

"Still, it would've saved a lot of time," Albert suggests.

"Time means nothing. Praise means nothing. Competing with others means nothing. What matters is only the task in front of you," Mr. Singerman advises. "You must give it *everything*. Everything."

"Mr. Singerman? Why are you crying?"

"I cry because my father cried, and his father cried. It's part of making a coffin. Some men don't cry, because they fear it's a sign of weakness. I was taught that a man's a man *because* he *can* cry."

Mr. Singerman takes Albert into the meadow, and they plant a tree together. He tells Albert that it's important not to take and take and take, but to give back as well. "God provided us with trees for a craftsman's livelihood, so we must plant some in return." He encourages Albert to keep asking questions in life and then search for the answers to them.

The lessons Albert learns during this special apprentice job are just as important as the work itself. I have found this to be true in real life, too. When I look back at the many jobs I've had, there are countless "take-aways," so many things gained in addition to the actual work.

With every job, we can learn just as much about life as we do about the skill we're practicing. When my children are old enough to begin working, I'll be sure to remind them to ask questions, search for answers, and look for the life lessons.

The tougher the fight, the more important the mental attitude.
—Michael Landon

Michael Landon holds Wendi and Brenda Turnbaugh on the set of *Little House.*
"Michael Landon, as a father figure, set the bar high." –Wendi Lou Lee
Photo courtesy of Wendi Lou Lee.

A photo I received in response to a fan letter I sent to Melissa Gilbert in 1980(ish). Melissa can't believe I've kept it all these years! Doesn't she realize how awesome she is? *Photo by permission of Melissa Gilbert.*

This is my Miss Beadle Bag, made by Charlotte Stewart! She does beautiful work . . . . And to top it off, she signed the bottom of it for me. *Photo by Alicia Murphy.*

I love my collection of Walnut Grove miniatures! These beautiful models are made by Bill and Jeanne Northum of Old West Miniatures. The detail and craftsmanship are fabulous! Check them out online! *Photo by permission of Bill and Jeanne Northum.*

Remember all the dinners we watched the Ingalls eat around their table in the little house over the years? The actors were eating Dinty Moore Beef Stew and Pillsbury biscuits! Guess what I fed my family on the night I was told that this book was "a go?" Prairie chow! Nuthin' ever tasted so good. *Photo by Alicia Murphy.*

The folks in my house aren't the only ones eatin' Walnut Grove-style! Pictured here are Lilyanna, Lily, Tommy, Evelyn, and Abby. These Little House fans from my hometown are all decked out in their prairie garb, having a picnic and "playing Little House." A third generation of viewers is loving – and I'm sure learning from - the show! *Photo courtesy of Laura Kuchler.*

Chapter 9
Sibling Rivalry

"I'm Getting' the Jealousies Again."

SIBLING RIVALRY. IT'S PRESENT IN JUST ABOUT every family at some point. The Ingalls are no different. The kids struggle with envy, differences of opinion, and competition for their parents' attention. The first big sibling rivalry situation I remember happening on *Little House* is in "The Love of Johnny Johnson" (season one). Laura falls head over heels for a country bumpkin who actually has his sights set on Mary.

Wanting Johnny to notice her, Laura "falls" into the creek deliberately one morning so that she can wear her pretty Sunday dress to school. She gets annoyed when Johnny sticks up for Mary at recess and also asks her to tutor him in reading.

At home, Laura says to Mary, "We used to always have fun walking home *(with Johnny).* Now all you do is show off playing teacher!"

"Don't be silly!" Mary says.

"I'm not being silly! And you're two-faced, Mary Ingalls, saying one thing behind Johnny's back and acting another to his face!"

"It wasn't my idea to play teacher. It was his!" Mary argues. "You're just a foolish-"

"Shut up! You just shut up!" Laura yells.

Whoa. Shut up? That's like cursing on the prairie.

*****

Unfortunately, this isn't the only time Laura will lose her love interest to her beautiful older sister. In "I'll Be Waving as You Drive Away" (season four), Laura strikes up a friendship with a good-looking, friendly young man named Seth. He walks her home and sees Mary outside. *Uh-oh.* Laura introduces them, and Seth asks if *Mary* would like to take a walk with him sometime. *Here we go again.*

That night, Mary says to Charles and Caroline, "I met a boy today."

"More like *stole* him," Laura says. "*I* saw him first."

"Don't you think he's a little *old* for you?" Mary says, condescendingly.

Sibling rivalry is NOT fun.

I have two sons and one daughter. My boys are three years apart, so I doubt we'll have competition between them for girls. They do, however, have their fair share of fights over Xbox controls and snuggle time with the dog. My daughter does not have a sister, but I have to level with you. I'm ***really*** *not looking forward to the drama that may ensue amongst her group of girlfriends when they start to become interested in boys. I may move to Mankato.*

*****

There are multiple shows in which Laura feels jealous of one of her siblings because she fears that one or both of her parents loves the other child more. "The Lord is My Shepherd" (season one) is one of *Little House's* most famous and popular episodes. This very emotional story begins with Caroline surprising Charles with the news that she's pregnant. I've always loved this scene.

"Sit down and have your lunch," Caroline says, placing Charles' plate on the table.

"Aren't you gonna eat something?" he asks.

"Carrie already had lunch, and I'm not hungry."

"You've been eating enough lately to keep a bird alive."

"I'll gain weight soon enough," Caroline tells him. "All when due."

"Don't tell me you're worried about weight! You take after your mother. There's no way in the world you're gonna gain any pounds."

"There's *one* way," Caroline argues happily.

"Well, if there is, I'd sure like to know what-" Charles stops. His head snaps up from his plate.

Caroline turns slowly toward him, then smiles a giggly smile. Charles flies into her arms.

He's so thrilled, he can't even finish his lunch. The joy on his face as he says, "A baby?" is just beautiful. Explaining that he's too excited to eat, he tells Caroline, "I love you!" and heads out the door to work. *Michael Landon and Karen Grassle had incredible chemistry in these roles.*

Laura begins right away to worry about the new baby, and over the next few months, she tries to convince her pa that she's as strong, fast, and tough as a boy.

When Caroline delivers a son, Laura is crushed and continues on her quest to prove to Charles that she's boy-like.

Dr. Baker visits the house because the baby isn't gaining weight. The family is concerned, and Caroline asks the girls to pray for him. Laura won't do it.

"Pa cares enough for all of us. That's all he cares about anymore . . . I asked God for a sister, and He didn't listen. So now I don't care."

Because my own kids tend to "lock horns," I've read a few articles about sibling rivalry. They all said that there's a great tendency for children in a family to be jealous of one another simply because of the struggle for their parents' love and attention. It makes sense, but it's a shame. My kids have accused me of having a favorite. I find this crazy, but kids can't understand a mother's love. I won't say that

I love all of my children the same way, because ***they're*** *not the same. They are each unique.* ***They*** *are different, so I* ***love*** *them all differently. I do love them all* ***equally;*** *there is not more love for one than there is for another. They are each a gift from God, and I consider them to be my greatest accomplishment in life. All we can do is love our children and let them know that they are our joy, our pride, and our legacy.*

*****

In chapter seven, I described Mary's struggles during the math examination in "The Pride of Walnut Grove." Well, Mary isn't the only one struggling in this episode. Laura, while she's happy for her sister, is feeling inadequate.

Charles tells Mary that he can't afford to send her on the trip, and Laura opens up to Mary. "I'm sorry . . . This may sound kinda silly, but when I found out that you couldn't go, I felt kinda glad inside . . . I guess I got kinda jealous, you bein' so smart and all. Ya know what I mean?"

"Yeah," Mary says. "I get jealous sometimes, too."

"Of *me*? Why would you be jealous of *me*?"

"I don't know. Sometimes I think Pa loves you more than he loves me."

"That's silly!"

"No sillier than you being jealous of some ole contest."

"You're right," Laura agrees. "Well anyway, I'm sorry about being jealous."

"Me too."

When the school board decides to pay to send Mary to the competition, Laura is happy, but her old feelings begin to creep back in. "I'm feeling kinda jealous again," she tells Charles as she puts Mary's bag in the wagon. "Mary can do lots of things! And I'm feeling useless."

Charles decides to boost Laura's confidence by telling Caroline that while she and Mary are away, he knows Laura will be able to take care of everything at the house. ***Great move, Pa! He makes the underdog feel important on what is a very big pomp-and-circumstance day for the hero.***

Laura puts her hair in a bun, like Caroline wears it. She speaks to Carrie the way her ma does and bakes a cake to surprise Mary. "I have to let it hang for an hour and a half," she says, turning it out of its pan. The cake crumbles.

"Oh, that's a shame," Pa says, helping her pick up the pieces from the floor. "It's not gonna hurt the taste of this part *(still in the pan)* anyway."

"Mary would've done it right," Laura says. "She does *everything* right . . . I wrecked the food, and I wrecked the cake. I just can't do anything! I bet you'll be glad when Ma gets back."

"Now you listen to me, young lady," says Charles. "You took care of this house, you did the cooking, the cleaning, everything! You took care of your sister. Why, any man would be proud to have you for a wife."

Bravo, Charlie Boy! Way to take a difficult situation and build your child up. Knowing that Laura's anticipation of Mary's return – and the town-wide praise that will most likely come with it – is making Laura feel inferior, Charles uses this moment to reassure her that she's awesome. He also points out that nobody's perfect. Parent-induced self-confidence in children is one of the best gifts we can give them. Pointing out their strengths and reminding them that their weaknesses only make them human can really give our kids a sense of stability. They need to know that they are not only good enough, but amazing!

*****

Similar to her feelings in "The Lord is My Shepherd," Laura is threatened by Albert's relationship with Charles in the episode "Fagin" (season five). She is happy that orphan Albert comes to Walnut Grove with her family when they return home from Winoka, but her happiness quickly turns to envy when her pa suddenly has a son. This episode begins with Charles giving Albert a baby calf (which he names Fagin) to raise.

"Hear that, Laura? I get to raise it!" Albert grins.

"Yeah, I heard." Laura is *not* grinning. She immediately knows that Charles will now be spending a lot of time with Albert and Fagin.

"When the Sleepy Eye fair rolls around, he's gonna bring a pretty good price at auction," Charles says.

"Don't worry, Mr. Ingalls! Fagin will win! I'm gonna make sure he has enough grain!" Albert says, heading outside.

"I better go with him," Charles says. "Otherwise he'll spend the whole night out in the barn."

"Pa! I forgot to show you!" Laura exclaims. "I got an A on my English test!"

"Hey! I knew you could do it. Why don't you clean up the table? Almost time for supper." Charles pretty much blows her off on his way out the door.

Laura looks at her test sadly. "It was the only A in the class."

As Fagin grows larger, so does Laura's jealousy. She watches as Albert and Charles work and laugh together. She's upset when Charles tells Albert to call him "Pa" (and of course, Nellie has to rub it in, causing Laura to haul off and deck her). When she finally breaks down in tears and opens up, Caroline is shocked by Laura's confession. Caroline hasn't noticed how much attention has been taken from Laura until now.

"Nobody cares about *me*," Laura sobs. "Nellie gets punched, everybody cares. Fagin gets sick, everybody cares."

"Laura, that's not true," Caroline tells her.

"Yes it is! I know it's true. And Albert – I thought he liked me. But it wasn't me he wanted. It was Pa. *MY* pa. He doesn't spend any time with me anymore. He's always with Albert and that stupid calf! And Albert – He calls him 'Pa.' But don't expect me to call him my brother, because he's isn't!"

Charles goes to Laura and ***admits his mistake***, telling her that when Albert came to live with them, he wanted to make sure Albert felt like he was part of the family. Charles explains that he spent extra time with him, assuming that Laura knew how much she was loved. He apologizes that he has taken her for granted.

Meanwhile, after overhearing Charles and Caroline talking, Albert decides to hit the road. Laura feels awful, knowing that her feelings are the reason he left.

This episode is a boo-hoo-er. It's also very realistic, because it shows not only

how sibling rivalry can get in the way of a happy family, but also how brothers and sisters can realize how much they love each other, when it comes right down to it. As much as my children fight, I know they'd miss each other (eventually!) if they weren't together.

"Fagin" also demonstrates that we can easily forget how important our attention and affection are to our children. Listening to them and even picking up on their silent cues will enlighten us to how they're feeling. Who knows? It may even decrease or prevent sibling rivalry a bit. If Charles had paid more attention to Laura, she would have felt more important.

If he had realized she wanted to help him and Albert while they were raising Fagin, she would have felt more included. If Charles and Caroline had picked up on her silent cues sooner, the whole conflict they dealt with may have been avoided. Just sayin.'

*****

When *Little House on the Prairie* became *Little House: A New Beginning*, the Ingalls had moved away, and the story focused more on Laura and Almanzo. A new family moved into the Ingalls' little house. "John and Sarah Carter" had two boys, named "Jeb" and "Jason," who carried on the same kinds of shenanigans and sibling rivalry we saw with the Ingalls children.

"The Last Summer" is another tear jerker. I cry every time I watch it. Jason, who is about 9 years old (and absolutely *adorable*, by the way) is envious of his brother Jeb (around 12 years old), who has a job. Their mother's birthday is coming up, and the boys are trying to decide what to get her.

"By the end of the week," Jeb says to John, "I'll have enough to get what I picked out *(in the catalog from the mercantile)*. "It's a birdfeeder. Jason, what are you gonna get Ma for her birthday?"

"I don't know," Jason says, rolling his eyes.

"Oh, we'll think of something, John says. "You could always get her a new washboard."

"That's what I gave her *last* year," Jason groans. "I wish I could get a gift myself, like Jeb."

A wealthy widow named "Ruthy Leland" comes to spend the summer in Walnut Grove. Jason is psyched when she offers him a job helping her butler with work around her house.

"Just give me a week," he tells Ruthy. "If I don't do good, you don't have to pay me! You can even fire me if you want!"

As promised, Jason works his tail off. In addition, Ruthy and her butler, Dewey, quickly come to adore him. Ruthy teaches Jason how to ride a horse properly and fish with a special fly rod. She also pays Jason quite well, which Jeb realizes during the church collection one Sunday morning.

"Jason, you put in two dimes. You know you only have to give one-tenth of what you make," Jeb says.

"I can do fractions."

"That lady gave you *two dollars?!*"

"You weren't supposed to watch!"

"Yeah, but *two dollars*!!" Suddenly, Jeb is the one who's feeling jealous and inferior. The sibling rivalry here is reciprocal.

The end of this episode is touching and sad. Ruthy has a wonderful bond with Jason (whose cuteness factor is off the charts!), but we learn that she is dying. Have your tissues ready if you watch this one! Ruthy writes Jason a beautiful letter, which he receives after she passes away:

> "You once said that you wished you were old. Well, Jason, don't be in any great rush; but live every day as if it were your last. Because the last ones can be so precious, as precious as you made mine. Jason Carter, I will cherish forever the memory of the summer I spent with you. I hope you will, too."
>
> *Love,*
>
> *Ruthy*

Sniffle, sniffle, wipe, wipe. Every. Single. Time.

David Freidman, our "Jason," shared with me his thoughts about this one: "My favorite episode, without a doubt, was "The Last Summer." I am honored to have been in just about every scene of that show. Vera Miles, who was a Hollywood legend, co-starred in that episode (as Ruthy). *There were some very touching scenes. As I grow older, I appreciate that episode more than ever! When I was on the show, I was very self-critical and thought I was a lousy actor. I would notice certain expressions, mannerisms and behaviors that would make me cringe. I was a self-inflicted perfectionist. Now, when I watch it, I get a kick out of myself and actually think I was a decent little actor. Some of the nuances I alluded to I now see in my own kids, and it makes me a proud dad!"*

Pamela Roylance ("Sarah") also recalls "The Last Summer" as her favorite. She described to me what a special episode it was for her, especially in her scenes with David. "He could melt you with one look," she shared. She and I agreed that he did a terrific job. We also talked about how we both cry every single time we watch this one. It was so touching, and the characters were absolutely endearing. Pam also has fond memories of working with Vera Miles and told me what an honor it was to share the stage with an actress of her caliber. She remembers vividly how Vera was able to bring just the right energy to the scene where Sarah has tea with Ruthy. This was a delicate part, and both Vera and Pam performed beautifully! After my conversation with Pam, I just had to watch "The Last Summer" again; and Pam told me later that she tuned into it that evening, too!

The sibling rivalry in "The Last Summer" has to do with money, which is pretty common. It's also pretty harmless. I remember as a kid, I always had lots of money because I saved everything I got. My brother spent his as soon as he had it, so I recall his envy whenever he saw my piggy bank. Being that he was older and smarter than I was, it always made me feel cool that I was richer. Hee hee hee . . .

*****

Jeb and Jason exhibit rivalry again in "Little House: The Last Farewell," the final episode (TV movie, actually) of the series. They have a rabbit-selling business together, and Jeb isn't keeping up his end of the bargain. "Hey Jason, I got somethin' I gotta do. Do you mind cleaning the cages without me?"

"Yeah, I mind!" Jason says, annoyed. "This rabbit business was your idea to begin with!"

"Well, come Easter, you're gettin' half the money, aren't you?"

"Yeah."

"Well then . . . Just do me this one favor. I wouldn't ask you if it wasn't important," Jeb says.

"Well, where are you going?"

"Jason, it's *so* important, I can't even tell you!"

"All right," Jason agrees. "But just this once."

"Thanks."

"C'mon, Jeb!" calls one of his friends. "Ya goin' swimming or not?"

Jason fumes. "Swimming?!?! Jeb! That's not fair! You said it was important! Jeb! Jeb!" he calls as his brother runs off with his friend. Jason grumbles, "I hope you get water in your ears! I hope you get sick and throw up!"

At home, he cleans the rabbit cages by himself. "My brother had something more important to do," he tells the rabbits. "He went swimming . . . Four more weeks 'til Easter, and then I won't have to take care of you guys anymore. And I'll have enough money to buy whatever I want!"

When (Pa) John hears where Jeb is, he tells Jason, "You shouldn't let him get away with that."

"I can't do nothin.' He's bigger than me. I wish you guys had me first."

"Just poor planning on our part I guess," John smiles.

"There *is* something you can do. I'd sure like it if you and Ma could make a younger child. Then it wouldn't be so bad if *I* had someone to pick on."

"Well, Son, I'm gonna have to talk to your ma about that."

"Oh, thanks, Pa! Ya hear that Herby?" Jason says to a rabbit. "Ma and

Pa might make another child! So then I could do what Jeb does to me. You know, hard pinchin,' and pickin' my nose and make him eat it . . . Aw, yeah. Lots of fun!"

Eeeeeeew.

John and Sarah have to go away on a trip in this episode, so Charles and Caroline stay in their old house and look after Jeb and Jason. One night, Jeb comes down from the loft and wakes them. Jason isn't in his bed, and Jeb is worried.

Charles finds Jason in the barn, talking to the rabbits.

"You have to understand," Jason is saying, "I need a way to make the money to buy stuff for my ma and pa. So they'll see that I'm grown up!"

"Jason," Charles interrupts, "you're not gonna grow at all if you don't get some sleep."

"What are you doing here, Mr. Ingalls?"

"Your brother woke me up. He was worried about you."

"He wasn't worried. He just wanted to get me in trouble."

"Aw, c'mon now, Jason. You don't believe that."

"I sure do! Don't take this wrong, Mrs. Ingalls, but I know my brother better than you do."

"Well, I'm sure you do Jason, but I still think he was worried about you."

"I guess you've never had an older brother."

"Now, hold on. That's where you're wrong. I did too."

"And he treated you nice?"

"Well, sometimes. Most of the time he told me what to do, because I was too little to do anything about it."

"You see? Older brothers are all alike. A bunch of bullies!"

"Well, ya know, sometimes I think they do it because they're scared."

"Scared of what?"

"Scared that maybe their ma and pa might love their little brother more than they do them."

"That's dumb."

"Now, I don't think so. Just think about it for a minute. I mean, here was your brother, he had the whole family all to himself, and along came you. You know how moms and pops are about little babies. I mean, they're pickin' 'em up all the time, tellin' 'em how cute they are, givin' 'em all that lovin.' That's enough to make a body get a little bit jealous, I think."

"Jealous. I never really thought of it that way. Do you really think he was worried about me?"

"I'm sure of it. Ya know what I think? I think you and I oughta get some sleep."

"You're right." Jason goes into the house with Charles, who is amused by their little talk.

He always knows just how to make kids feel better. I guess when we look back at our own childhoods and put ourselves in our kids shoes, it can help us relate to them; and, in turn, help them.

In the loft, Jason wakes Jeb up.

"Jason, I'm sleeping. What do you want?"

"I just wanna tell you not to be jealous."

"What do you mean?"

"Ya know, being jealous because Ma and Pa love me more than they do you. I'm sure they don't. But thanks for worrying about me."

"I don't know what you're talking about. And I *wasn't* worried about you."

"Aw, c'mon. Sure you were! Why else would you wake up Mr. Ingalls and have him come look for me?"

" 'Cause I thought he'd give it to ya good, that's why. Now go to sleep!"

Jason gets into his bed, saying to himself, "Why do kids listen to grownups?"

Fun scene. I love how Charles hits the nail on the head when he "diagnoses" Jeb, and then Jeb acts too cool to admit that he really is kind of jealous of Jason sometimes. Again, I wish kids could understand a parents' love for their children. On the other hand, I guess it's only human for siblings to have some competitive rivalry between them. It's all part of growing up! As a parent, on the other hand

(I think I've run out of hands), I could surely do without all the fighting. In my parenting book,* MOTHERHOOD: Insert Humor Here, *there's a whole chapter about "sibling quibbling." If only I could figure out a solution to this eternal, universal problem . . . I'd be the hero of hero township.

I'm not the kind of person who gives up without a fight.
—Michael Landon

Chapter 10
Having Selfless Concern for —and Giving to—Others

"I Wanted to Buy Ma a Stove for Christmas."

One of the greatest things we can teach our children is compassion for others. Having genuine concern for our neighbors is an admirable trait, and giving to another person without expecting anything in return is a wonderful act. These ideas are presented repeatedly in *Little House on the Prairie.* In the episode "Town Party, Country Party" (season one), Laura befriends "Olga," who was born with one leg shorter than the other. When Laura hurts her ankle at Nellie's birthday party, Olga comforts her. The two girls hang out together while the others play. Laura notices that when Olga steps up onto a low log with her short leg, she can walk normally. When she tells Charles about this, he offers to make Olga a special shoe, hoping it will eliminate her limp.

Olga's pa is stubborn and protective, refusing Charles' offer. However, her grandmother brings Charles one of Olga's shoes and gratefully requests that he try to construct a new one. Charles is able to do it, and as Olga walks for the first time without limping, tears of joy run down her face. She collapses into Charles' arms with a hug of gratitude as Laura and the rest of the family look on. What a moment!

Charles and Laura have both given selflessly to Olga; Laura by offering her friendship, and Charles by making the shoe. These actions have changed this little girl's life. And it cost the Ingalls nothing. This is such an awesome lesson in kindness, compassion, and including those who have differences. I love it!

Olga's father comes to the Ingalls' house to have it out with Charles for going against his wishes and taking Olga's shoe. He is physically fighting with Charles when he sees his daughter running and playing happily with the other girls. He can't believe it and is overcome with emotion. It's beautiful when he hugs his joy-filled daughter. ***Gotta love a happy ending, especially one created by selfless people!***

*****

"Christmas at Plum Creek" (season one) is all about selfless giving. This is such an uplifting one! Each member of the Ingalls family is concerned in his or her own way about what to get the others for Christmas. Every one of them comes up with perfect ideas, and they don't care how hard they have to work or what they have to sacrifice to obtain those gifts.

Both Laura and Charles notice Caroline eyeing up the stove on display at the mercantile. Charles makes a deal with Nels to refinish a set of buckboard wheels in order to buy the stove. Both Mary and Caroline know that Charles needs a new shirt. Even little Carrie has seen a silver star that she wants to get for the top of their Christmas tree.

Caroline is able to buy the fabric for Charles' shirt and sews it when he's not in the house. Mary buys the same fabric (unbeknownst to both of them) and makes the shirt with the help of the town seamstress. Carrie looks in her special box and finds a penny she thinks she can use to buy the silver star.

Laura struggles at first about how to afford her gifts. Then she comes up with a brilliant idea. Knowing how much Nellie envies her pony, Laura offers to trade it to Nels in exchange for the stove. *Wow! That's what I call love. She is thinking completely of her mother and not herself.*

On Christmas Day, Caroline is confused when the shirt Mary gives Charles looks identical to the one that she, herself, has made for him. She tucks hers under the Christmas tree skirt, so as not to take away from Mary's hard work. *Selfless.* Laura loves the saddle her pa made for her horse, though she knows she won't be able to use it. Caroline is delighted with her stove but shocked (as is Charles!) when the card is signed "Laura." Just then, Nels and Nellie arrive to pick up the pony.

Caroline wants to stop Laura from giving her horse to Nellie, but Charles reminds her, "She had the right."

"But she loves Bunny so," Caroline argues.

"She loves you more," Charles says.

"Oh, I can't-" Caroline frets.

"Caroline, she wants to do this. She loves you. Don't spoil it for her."

Laura comes back into the house crying, and Caroline hugs her so tightly. "I just love my stove!" she tells her. "Don't cry. Someday we'll have another pony."

"It's not the pony," Laura says. She looks at Charles. "I'm sorry about all the work you had to do on the saddle, Pa."

So selfless. *Can we all have a Laura? This has always been one of my favorite episodes. First of all, anything having to do with the holiday season can put me in a good mood; but then to see the messages and lessons about giving? It never gets old. Joy to the world!*

*****

"At the End of the Rainbow" (season two) is a feel-good, fantasy-filled episode. Laura and her friend Jonah are fishing one day when they spot something shiny in the creek. They're sure it's gold! Right away, they make a pact to keep it a secret between them, and they plan to collect all the gold so they can become rich and surprise their families.

Laura and Jonah spend weeks gathering their treasure. In the meantime, Laura has the most amazing dreams about the Ingalls' life as a wealthy family, living in a castle and wearing fancy clothing. Laura imagines her family owning the whole town of Walnut Grove, which is so entertaining! *Each time I watch this episode, I think how fun it must've been for the cast to film it. Those who played the Ingalls got to wear beautiful formal wear, and their hair was all fancy. The actors who played the Olesons dressed in old, ratty clothes for once. It was probably a fun change of pace for the actors!*

When Laura and Jonah have bagged all of their "gold," they play hooky from school one day so they can take it all to the bank. Sadly, the banker tells them that what they've found isn't gold, but instead iron pyrite (which is worth nothing).

"Oh Pa," Laura cries later, "I was gonna give you so much! I was gonna buy Ma all she wanted at Olesons, and I was gonna buy you a big house and everything! And now look at it."

"Half-Pint, you listen to me," Charles says. "You give us everything we want every single day of our lives. You give us love, respect, and joy. There isn't enough gold in the whole world to

buy those things."

Laura smiles. "It was kinda nice dreaming about it."

"Well, sure it was! That's what dreams are for!"

Through all of her daydreams, night dreams, and every dream in between, Laura never thought of or mentioned buying anything for herself. It was all about what she wanted to give to the rest of her family. Of course, all kids would plan to get themselves something; but those things weren't foremost in Laura's mind. First, she wanted to give everything to her family. What a sweet message for our young people.

*****

Speaking of "sweet," the love story of Charles and Caroline over the years is the *sweetest*. Theirs is a relationship filled with mutual adoration for each other. Their strong bond carries them through the worst of times and makes them even more thankful for one another during happy moments. Charles and Caroline give to each other – and to their children – selflessly, always wanting what's best for everyone else.

Charles demonstrates such selfless giving in "For My Lady" (season two). He and Mary deliver a set of new china to a beautiful widow who has hired Charles to build a cabinet for her dishes. Living alone in the huge home her late husband built for her, "Mrs. Thurman" has exquisite taste (and a kind personality as well). Charles and Mary admire her lovely new china.

"What will you do with the old set?" Mary asks.

"Oh, probably store them until somebody comes along and wants to buy them," Mrs. Thurman answers.

"Ma sure would like them!" Mary suggests.

"Mary, mind your manners." Charles tells her.

"Well, Mr. Ingalls, if you think your wife would truly like them, I'd be happy to accept your work on the cabinet as payment," Mrs. Thurman agrees. "You can take them with you!"

"I appreciate that very much, but, to be very honest with you, we need the money right now, a lot more than we do the dishes."

At home, Mary describes Mrs. Thurman's new china, and Caroline is intrigued. Charles becomes uncomfortable, hearing them talk about something he can't provide.

That night, Caroline admires Charles' work on the cabinet.

"Well, I wish I was doing it for *you*," Charles tells her.

She assures him that there are a lot of things they need more. "Right now, I'd settle for a little more time with you," Caroline says. *LOVE this.*

Charles works hard at Mrs. Thurman's house to finish the cabinet. While there, he notices some damaged woodwork in the dining room. "I'll tell you what," he says. "I'll redo your woodwork in exchange for your old set of dishes." He wants to make Caroline happy with a surprise. *So romantic!*

This is a sweet love story. As all the buzz flies around town (and even enters

Caroline's imagination) about the possible "goings-on" between Charles and another woman, he is working his butt off to buy something for the only woman he truly loves. He puts in countless hours just so he can give selflessly to his wife and make her happy. The best kind of reward is seeing those we love feel joy. All the more reason to teach our children to practice giving without expecting anything in return.

*****

In "Freedom Flight" (season four), Charles and Dr. Baker offer aid when a Native American arrives in Walnut Grove seeking medical care for his ailing father. He comes in peace but doesn't receive it in return from some of the bigots in town. Because of such hatred, Charles agrees to invite the Native American father and his family to hide in the Ingalls' sod house so they won't be harmed. He says to Mary, "They may not read the same bible we do or worship God in the same way, but they're His children, too." This is his reason for giving selflessly to these people; they're suffering and starving. He just wants to help.

"Mr. MacGregor," one of said haters, finds out that the family is there. He rounds up all of his friends so they can come to the Ingalls' farm and kill the Native Americans.

In a mad rush to get the endangered family to safety, Charles and Dr. Baker load them into Charles' wagon and rush out of town.

The other men enter the Ingalls' house and threaten Caroline. She stands tall and still, staring straight ahead.

"I'm losing my patience now," Mr. MacGregor tells her after a while. "I can *make* you tell me if I have to."

Caroline's eyes shift to his for the first time. "Mr. MacGregor. If you lay a hand on me, you'd better be sure you have a lot of help."

MacGregor is shocked by this response. She stares him down.

Yeah, Caroline!

Meanwhile, Charles crosses paths with another wagon in the middle of the prairie and comes up with a great idea. He offers to trade his wagon for the other guy's broken down rig. This throws off MacGregor and his men. They follow the wrong set of tracks, giving Charles and Dr. Baker more time to get the Native Americans to safety.

This lesson in selfless giving has been brought to you by the words "love" and "compassion." We don't need reasons to care for one another, other than it's the right thing to do. A wonderful message for our kids! I talk frequently to mine about doing random acts of kindness. Such a simple way to make a difference in our world, and who doesn't enjoy making someone else happy? I try to encourage this by doing acts of kindness regularly. If my children see me doing so, hopefully it will make them want to follow.

*****

"The Inheritance" (season four) is an episode in which Charles and Caroline give an awful lot but don't receive anything in return (until the end, when they get a whopper of a gift!). The story begins with Charles receiving word that a very wealthy uncle he barely remembers has passed away and left Charles his entire estate. The Ingalls can't believe it and begin to get excited about the new life this money could create for them. Not wanting to get too serious until the money is actually in their hands, they go about their everyday lives. Their friends are envious – jealous even – of their newfound wealth. Jonathan Garvey breaks business plans with Charles, figuring he won't need the work once he's rich. Andy Garvey gets snippy with Laura when he assumes she soon won't have time for things like the clubhouse they've been building together. Harriet Oleson begins treating Caroline like a queen, now that the Ingalls (almost) have money to their name.

Charles is hit up by the school to purchase books for the annual book drive. Reverend Alden stops over one night and asks if the Ingalls will buy a church organ for Sunday services. Charles and Caroline are thrilled to be able to provide such things for their town; they're happy to give to their friends and neighbors. Though Charles reminds everyone that he hasn't seen any of the money yet, his friends keep asking for more. The Olesons extend credit to him until his bill at the mercantile is so high that they need to require payment. Charles is forced to sign a lien on his farm in case he doesn't pay for all the purchased items.

Things go south when the Ingalls learn that the uncle's enormous debt has wiped out the entire estate. Charles and Caroline are left with nothing. Mrs. Oleson arranges for their property and all of their belongings to be auctioned. Needless to say, the Ingalls are devastated.

Leading up to this point, their friends have made requests out of greed and have distanced themselves from the Ingalls out of envy. With the exception of Harriet, they all feel guilty for placing so much pressure on Charles and Caroline and for being selfish. As a result, they decide (again with the exception of Harriet) to come up with a plan to save them.

When his wife heads out to the Ingalls' house with the auctioneer, Nels stands on the main road in Walnut Grove and tells anyone coming in from out of town that the auction has been canceled. This leaves only the Ingalls' closest friends to participate in the purchasing. Every item mentioned by the auctioneer – including the farm, house, and barn – gets no more than two cents in the auction; the small group starts each round of bidding at one penny and goes no higher than two.

In the end, they all go into the Ingalls' house to tell them what they've done. "It all comes to about six cents if you want to buy it back," Jonathan says. "And you don't have to worry about cash, 'cause your credit's good with us, Charles." They apologize for how they've acted. After all, here were Charles and Caroline giving selflessly, just to give, and their friends were alienating

them. "It wasn't you who changed," Jonathan continues. "It was all of us around you." Everyone makes amends, and we have a happy ending that ***gives*** me a smile each time I watch it!

*****

Most of these examples of selfless giving have been acts made by the adults on *Little House*. How about the kids? Several episodes come to mind. In season three, there was one called "Little Women," in which a bitter widow blows off a friendly suitor, because she is too afraid of being hurt again. Time after time, she turns down his offers of kindness and companionship. Her daughter, "Ginny," who adores this nice man, is distraught. Her mother never leaves the house and won't even come to any of the functions at school.

When Miss Beadle plans a special day for all the parents to come in and watch the children perform short plays, Ginny is grouped with Laura and Mary. Nellie forces her way into the group when she hears them mention doing the play *Little Women.* She announces that her mother can write the script, and all the rehearsals can be at her house. *Hoo-ray*, think the girls. *Sarcasm intended.*

Ginny is so excited and begs her ma to come see her in the play. Her mother wearily declines, saying there's just too much to be done around the house, and that she wouldn't have a decent dress to wear. Ginny is again disappointed.

Rehearsals for *Little Women* are underway at the Olesons,' and Nellie has the lead. *I know. It's hard to believe. Again, sarcasm intended.* Harriet even orders her a *(hideous)* wig *(which she pays to have curled, making it doubly hideous!).* When the wig maker relays to the girls how much he pays women to let him cut their hair, Ginny gets an idea.

On the day of the big play, she presents her mother with a beautiful dress and begs her once more to put it on and come see the performance at school. Knowing that Ginny could never afford to buy such a dress, her mother accuses her of accepting it from the gentleman who is still trying to "court" her. She gets angry, telling Ginny to return the dress.

When "Mr. Mayfield" (the suitor) finds Ginny crying by the side of the road, he goes to set her mother straight. He basically instructs her to get her ass in gear, get her ass into the dress, and get her ass to the schoolhouse. *Nicely done, Sir.*

Ginny is thrilled when she sees her mother and Mr. Mayfield in the audience at school. The girls begin their performance, and the story of *Little Women* takes on a life of its own.

Nellie talks through the plotline of Jo contributing toward the father's health and helping with his return home. "I wonder how you could have gotten it *(the money)*. I hope you didn't beg, borrow, or steal it. Let me see, however could you have done it?" Nellie walks over and removes Ginny's bonnet, revealing a *(really bad)* short haircut. "Oh my!" she says, still in character, "You cut your hair!"

The other girls step out of character immediately. Questioned by Laura and Mary, Ginny explains, "It's only hair; it'll grow back." She also shares that she wanted to buy her mother a new dress "so she could come here today."

It means more to this little girl for her mother to be happy, feel beautiful, and spend time with other adults than it does for her own self to have a head of gorgeous, long hair (which, in those days, according to Charles Ingalls, was a "woman's crowning glory").

Any mother can appreciate – and sob over – this little girl's desire to see her mother try to relax and enjoy herself. Ginny's willingness to give anything so her mother can rediscover her life is so touching.

Our kids really do notice – and care – when we aren't present for their big moments. Things which may seem simple to us are huge to them. They live for our attendance at (and approval of) their school events, sports, concerts, and recitals. All we have to do is show up and be proud. Sounds like a win-win to me!

*****

Laura and Albert team up a few times to do kind, selfless things for others. In "The Third Miracle" (season six), the family learns that Mary's husband, "Adam," has been the first blind person chosen to receive the Louis Braille Award for his excellence in teaching. He and Mary are invited to attend the award ceremony in St. Paul. Adam is thrilled but announces that they can't afford to take the trip.

At dinner that night, Caroline explains the situation to Charles. "It's a once in a lifetime honor for Adam. They just don't have the money."

"Caroline, I'd do anything to help them; you know that. But we don't have it either. At least not that kind of money, anyway. Sixty dollars. There's just no way I could swing it."

Laura and Albert exchange looks as their parents are talking. They're on the same page. They've been jarring honey from a huge beehive by the creek, and they've made a deal with Nels to sell him the honey for $57.60. They've already dreamed about how they'll each spend their share of the money; Albert wants a velocipede, and Laura wants to buy a whole new outfit (to impress Almanzo). Selflessly, they choose to give their earnings to Adam and Mary instead.

Charles and Caroline are shocked. "You two worked a long time for that money," Charles says.

Caroline smiles. "Doing this for Mary and Adam is the best present you could give us. I'm so proud of you!"

And proud she should be. What a gift! For two kids to make that selfless decision on their own? Fantastic. Though the gift is monetary, Laura and Albert's desire to sacrifice their own material wishes in order to provide a rare opportunity for their sister and brother-in-law is the ultimate example of selflessness.

*****

We see this same dynamic duo work together for the sake of someone else's happiness in the episode "The Odyssey" (season five). Laura and Albert's friend, "Dillon," is an avid painter who longs to someday see the ocean. His home is filled with artwork he's created, all depicting the sea. The boy has promised his deceased father that he will one day go to the ocean and see it for himself. This doesn't seem like a difficult promise to keep until he finds out that he has leukemia.

With only a short time to live, Dillon decides he has to keep his promise to his pa.

He tells Laura and Albert, "I'm going to see the ocean," he shares. "I have to do it now. I'm gonna die."

Laura and Albert decide to go with Dillon. Though they know the trip will be nearly 2,000 miles and very difficult (and they'll probably get the whippings of their lives when they get home), they feel it's important to help their friend realize his dream and keep his promise to his father.

This is one kind of journey I wouldn't necessarily recommend to my kids. Lol. But I do encourage them to help others in any way they possibly can, whether it's helping someone pick up something they've dropped or helping a friend find his dream! Giving without getting is its own reward!

*****

In season eight of *Little House*, Laura is grown up, married, pregnant, and teaching in Walnut Grove. She and Almanzo have planted an apple orchard on their farm, which they hope will provide them with the money they need to buy more land. All is going well, and the orchard is growing beautifully.

In this episode called "Stone Soup," Charles and Almanzo are offered $300 to haul mining equipment to northern Arizona. They decide it's an opportunity they can't pass up, and Laura insists she'll be able to take care of herself and the orchard for the two months Almanzo will be gone. What she doesn't realize is that a heat spell and a drought are on the way. *Ugh! No A/C and no sprinkler systems in the 1880's . . .*

As weeks pass with no rain, the townspeople are worried about their crops. Between teaching, farming the orchard, and taking care of her house, Laura completely exhausts herself. She arrives late to work, falls asleep in class, and has worked her hands until they're blistered and bloody. Caroline tries to reason with her but has no success. Laura continues to work until she literally collapses from a heat stroke.

Caroline takes over as teacher while Laura recovers. While in the classroom, she tells the kids a story called "Stone Soup." It's about a starving British solider during the American Revolution who arrives in a small village and knocks on all the doors asking for food and shelter.

Everyone tells him they have no food to share, and no one welcomes him in. The soldier decides to trick them into contributing ingredients for a big pot of soup that the entire community can share. The soldier's plan works, and everyone enjoys a great meal together.

When Caroline finishes, she says to the class, "If you're waiting for me to tell you what the story means, you'll just have to figure it out for yourselves." She leaves the children there to think.

"I guess it means it's important to help each other," Albert says.

"There's something more to the story besides just helping people," Willie adds. "It's like a lot of people, all working together to get something done."

That afternoon, Laura laments the dying trees. "If only I could have saved the orchard."

"It was too much for one body to do," Caroline reminds her. "But it's not too much for a *lot* of people to do!" She and Laura see all the kids from school approaching with their buckets.

"We'll save your trees for you, Mrs. Wilder!" Willie says. The kids run off to the pond to fill their buckets. They water the entire orchard and then talk about who else they may be able to help. "Ya know Mrs. Ingalls," Willie says, "this working together – it kinda makes you feel good!"

The children had no obligation to help Laura (or any of the townspeople). They wanted to. They learned from Caroline's story that if everyone teams up, an awful lot can get accomplished. More importantly, they learned that it can even be fun when they're all together doing something meaningful. Random acts of kindness and selfless concern for others – I highly recommend them!

I believe that there is God in all of us.
—Michael Landon

Chapter 11
Being Honest with Yourself

"In the Name of God, Stop Pretending!"

As parents, we all try to instill honesty and integrity in our kids. We want our children to grow up to be trusted because they speak the truth and are loyal to others. Just as important, though, is a loyalty to self. There are so many times in life when we have to remind ourselves and our children to be honest within. This can be a really painful thing to do, especially when things like success, achievement, and even dreams are at stake. Sometimes, we go so far as to convince ourselves that we're doing something for the good of someone else when really, we're doing it for our own satisfaction.

An example of this is found in "The Enchanted Cottage" (season five), an episode that begins with Mary teaching at the blind school when she's suddenly distracted by "light." She stops several times during her lesson and turns toward the window, where the sunshine is beaming in. Convinced she is regaining her eyesight, she begins to dream about all the things that she and Adam will be able to do now.

Charles takes Mary to the city to have her eyes examined. At first, the doctor feels there may be hope, but upon further examination, he finds that there is no sign of improvement. *The scene is heartbreaking. Charles stays in the exam room to watch as the doctor shines a very bright light on Mary's face. Each time he does so, he asks if she can see it. Each time, she answers, "Yes." Then he tells her he is taking the light off of her face, but he leaves it on. He asks her to describe what she's seeing, and she says, "Nothing now, but I could see the light." The look on Charles' devastated face kills me every time.* The doctor explains to him that, for Mary to "see the light," all it took was the warmth of sunshine on her face or the suggestion that a light was there for her mind to produce it.

Charles has the awful job of telling Mary that there's no chance at all. On their way home, they talk some more. "I hate going back," Mary tells him. "It's not because of me. It's Adam. I know how this must hurt him."

Charles takes a deep breath. "Well, I think the first thing you oughta do starting right now is start being honest with yourself and stop pretending that it's Adam you feel sorry for."

Mary is stunned. "But it is," she tries to convince him (and herself).

"It's not," Charles answers. "You're feeling sorry for *yourself.* I can't say that I blame you, but stop lying to yourself about it."

"I'm not," Mary says. "It *is* Adam."

"It's Adam," Charles shoots back. "All right, if you had a choice . . . and one of you could see again, who would you pick? Would you pick you or Adam?"

"I don't know-"

"Aw, c'mon Mary, you'd pick yourself and you know it! And you wouldn't be doing it for Adam. I mean, in the name of God, just say it one time. I wanted to see again for me. Just say it. I wanted to see again for ***me***!"

Mary cries. "I wanted to see again for me."

This is a great scene. As hard as it is, even for Charles to deal with the facts, he makes sure that Mary is adjusting to the idea that she'll never see again; and he's making her be completely honest with herself about it. That takes a great

deal of courage and strength. As parents, it's important for us to remind our children to be true to themselves inside.

*****

A similar conversation between a parent and her child is staged in an episode named "Dearest Albert, I'll Miss You" (season seven). In school, Laura sets the class up with pen pals in Minneapolis, and Albert gets to write to a girl named "Leslie." He's very impressed with her exciting life in the city and her stories about dancing in the ballet and playing basketball; so impressed, in fact, that he feels like his own life is boring in comparison. As a result, Albert decides to fabricate exciting details when he writes back. He tells her he's the tall, popular captain of the football team.

What Albert doesn't know is that Leslie is making up the "facts" in her letters as well. In reality, she is in a wheelchair and can't participate in athletics. At her next check up with her doctor, Leslie's mother is told that there is no hope that Leslie will ever walk again. She knows, then, that it's time to level with her daughter, so that they can both get on with their lives.

"Have you written anything *(to Albert)* about your accident?" she asks Leslie that night.

"No."

"Don't you think you should?"

"I don't know. I really haven't thought about it. Besides, there are so many other things I want to write about," Leslie says.

"Like what?" her mother pushes. "Like the things you wrote in your last letter? I saw it on your desk. I know I shouldn't have looked at it, but I did."

"I wish you hadn't," Leslie says uncomfortably.

"I know," her mother nods. "Captain of the basketball team? Dancing in the school ballet?"

"Well, I *did* those things."

"You *did*!"

"And I'll do them again!" Leslie dreams. "I'm getting better all the time, and by the time I see Dr. Marx next month, I'll-"

Her mother stops her. "You won't be seeing Dr. Marx next month."

"Why not? Why not, Mother?!"

"We've got to stop pretending! Both of us! You're *not* getting better!"

"I am. The feeling was stronger than ever today!"

"You *want* to feel something, but you don't."

"I *do*!"

"You don't! I've known it from the beginning, Dr. Marx has known it from the beginning, and so have you. In the name of God, stop pretending! There are so many things you can do with your life. So many. But you won't do them if you keep waiting for a miracle to happen. Don't keep waiting for it to be as it was."

Leslie isn't the only one who learns to be honest with herself in this episode. Albert takes a lesson from it, too. Honesty is the best policy; with others and with ourselves. I love how, in addition to a parent imparting wisdom in this episode, two kids also learned from each other the importance of honesty. Good stuff!

Countless *Little House* episodes give us this advice about keeping ourselves in check. Poor Dr. Baker (in "Doctor's Lady," season one) and Mr. Edwards (in "Love," season nine) both have to make the difficult decision not to marry the young girl with whom they've fallen in love. Sadly for each, they are too old for said young girl and recognize that she has the right to have children with a husband who isn't old enough to be her father. They are honest with themselves, even when it's extremely painful to be.

Hester Sue, who teaches at the blind school with Mary and Adam, has tough choices to make when she finds herself engaged to one man but in love with another ("Make a Joyful Noise," season seven). The one she's supposed to marry is financially stable, but that's about all he has to offer.

"Do you love Hertzell?" Mary asks Hester Sue. "Can you honestly say you do?"

"Well, no," she answers. "I mean, not now, but it will come in time, and I would be a good wife."

"Nobody could be a good wife to a man she doesn't love," Mary argues.

"But, Mary, I said all of that will come in time."

Mary knows the truth. "It's Joe, isn't it?"

"Oh, what are you talkin' about?"

"I think *he's* the one you love. You just won't admit it."

"No!"

"Hester Sue, I'm your friend!" Mary says. "And *I* love you. If you can't admit that to me . . . Just admit it. You love Joe Kagan."

Hester Sue starts to cry. "All right. I love him." She goes on to explain how deeply she loved her first husband and how he drank and gambled away everything she worked for.

Meanwhile, there is a little blind boy at the school who thinks he that he doesn't need to do all the things the other blind children have to do, because he believes his eyesight is coming back soon. Nothing his teachers say to him can convince him otherwise. Joe Kagan is the only one who eventually gets through to him when he finally brings out the boy's anger toward his parents for "letting him go blind" and leaving him at the blind school. The boy bursts into tears and lets out all of his feelings. From there, he begins to accept and work through his new reality.

Hester Sue isn't ready to acknowledge her true feelings until her actual wedding day. Mary refuses to attend the ceremony knowing that Hester Sue doesn't love the guy, and then "the guy" himself is rude and ornery during the ceremony. Right then and there, she calls off the wedding and gives Joe a chance.

Sometimes it's our friends who bring us to our senses and help us to be honest with ourselves. Friends like these are keepers! Encouraging our kids to gravitate toward others who will have their backs and keep their best interests in mind is something to consider for sure. My son went to a summer basketball camp at my alma mater, Villanova University, and Coach Jay Wright invited former coach, Rollie Massimino, to speak. His advice to the kids was, "Surround yourself with good people." This simple message is golden.

*****

"Jenny Wilder" in *Little House: A New Beginning* encounters a special friend who helps her to overcome adversity and be honest with herself. In "Marvin's Garden" (season nine), an elderly doctor who lives in Walnut Grove, realizes that he has to stop practicing medicine, because he's losing his eyesight. This is an agonizing decision for him, but he knows it's necessary.

When Jenny is involved in a swimming accident that leaves her partially paralyzed, "Dr. Marv" takes Jenny on as his last patient. She feels comfortable with him and enjoys working with him in his greenhouse. The doctor absolutely loves her company as they tend to his many plants, rescue an injured bird, and talk about life. Jenny's speech and movement grow stronger every day, and before long, it's time for her to return to school.

The other kids are all excited to see Jenny and give her a warm welcome. Then Nancy decides to be her usual, bitchy self. She asks the teacher, "Can Jenny tell us what it was like almost drowning and all?"

With everyone staring at her, Jenny stands up and begins to tell her story. She struggles to pronounce some of her words, and the children are stunned. One giggles. Jenny is self-conscious and scared. Nancy watches with her obnoxious smirk.

At recess, Nancy continues to be evil. "I hate running in these shoes," she says, plopping down on the ground next to Jenny, who is sitting on a swing. "They pinch my feet. It's a shame you can't play. It must be awful. You were the best girl player in the school. I don't think I'd wanna live if something like that happened to me. I couldn't believe it when you started talking this morning. I mean, we all knew you weren't feeling well, but . . . Do you really think you'll get better?" Heading back out to the baseball game, Nancy adds, "You're lucky you *can't* play."

So mean! She definitely filled Nellie's shoes; or should I say Nellie's lace-up boots?

Jenny is so hurt and feels extremely isolated. She goes to see Dr. Marv. Running into his arms, she stutters, "Dr. Marv, it was awful. They acted so different, and Nancy said things that hurt me. I don't ever want to go back there again. I wanna stay here with you."

"All right, all right," says Dr. Marv. "Now, that's enough tears. So, you went back to school and they acted different to ya, is that it?'

"Yes," Jenny says.

"And you weren't different? You weren't any different than the way you were before? Of course you were."

"But, they made me feel uncomfortable," Jenny struggles.

"That's because *they* were uncomfortable. They didn't know what to say to you. Landsakes, you gotta give people a chance."

"But, Nancy said things-"

"Nancy said things to you?" Dr. Marv agrees. "Didn't she always? Didn't she?"

"Well, yes, but-"

"But what?" Dr. Marv says. "She shouldn't be mean to ya now because of what happened to ya? That's nonsense. You were upset with the other children because they acted differently. You were upset with Nancy because she acted the way she always does!"

Jenny is miserable. She's offended and hurt. "I thought you would understand," she says, heading for the door.

"What are you gonna do now, go home and feel sorry for yourself? That'll do you a lot of good," Dr. Marv pushes.

"You don't understand!" Jenny cries. "You pretended to be my friend! But you don't care!" Now screaming, "You don't care at all!"

"That's it! That's it! Get angry! It's good for ya!" Dr. Marv cheers. ". . . Use it! Fight this thing! Show Nancy! Show 'em all!"

Dr. Marv was a good friend and confidant to Jenny. He treated her delicately when she was first injured and then adjusted his approach as she became stronger. This is a key combination. My college roommates, Suzanne and Jen, have always been loyal in this way. Whenever I've struggled with something in my life, they have tried to see it from my perspective and support me in the

greatest ways possible. But when it's time for me to move on with things, they've always kicked me in the butt and told me to get going. Solid friends.

These aren't bad traits to encourage in our children! There are moments when we have to give ourselves – and others – the time needed to wallow a bit in our own sorrow. But after a short while, another important era has to begin: the era of being honest with ourselves and moving on.

Fun fact: During this episode, we can hear the music that later became the theme song of Michael Landon's show, Highway to Heaven. David Rose was the composer for Bonanza, Little House, and Highway. In fact, in some Bonanza episodes, we can find music that Rose eventually used in Little House. He did beautiful work. "I declare!" The heartwarming writing of Little House combined with the emotional melodies of David Rose? They really knew how to pull at our heartstrings! No wonder Little House fans could keep the Kleenex company in business.

Hersha Parady ("Alice Garvey") told me about a time she had to do some looping for a certain episode (looping is a postproduction process in which actors add or re-record dialogue to already-recorded footage while watching it on a screen). She said, "I walked into the studio, and there was ***David Rose with his entire orchestra*** *and a* ***HUGE*** *picture of my face on the big screen! Oh my God!" she laughed about it, and we went on to talk about the amazing musical creations of David Rose. It must've been cool to work with a whole orchestra like that (even if scary to see the* ***biggest selfie ever*** *on screen . . . Hersha had no idea that she was way ahead of her time)!*

*****

In "Marvin's Garden," Dr. Marv has to use tough love with Jenny so that she can start *to love herself* enough to be honest with herself and move on. There's an episode of *Little House* in which the *child* actually gives this needed tough love butt-kicking to the *parent*. ***An interesting twist!*** We remember the Ingalls' time living in the city of Winoka. They've moved there because Mary has joined Adam at a new blind school, and the economy in Walnut Grove is so bad that no one can make a living there, anyway. In order to keep their family together, Charles and Caroline are enduring the noise, chaos, and crappy working conditions of the city. They hate it there but are making the most of their new reality.

When it gets to the point where life in Winoka is absolutely tearing them up inside ("There's No Place Like Home," season five), Caroline shares her feelings with Charles. "Why do people have to have something to look forward to? That's the trouble with folks here. They're always looking forward to tomorrow, but missing today . . . And hurrying to make more and more money to buy something better tomorrow. But tomorrow never comes . . . You wanna go home, don't you?"

"No," Charles lies.

"You do. We *all* do."

"Well, we can't. It wouldn't be fair to Mary. There's nothing for her in Walnut Grove. She's gotta teach. We can't ask her to give that up."

"Charles," we wouldn't ask her to give it up," Caroline says.

"We're a family. We stay together."

"Charles-"

He cuts her off. "Things are gonna get better. You wait and see."

"Something better?" Caroline says sarcastically. "Tomorrow." She heads for the stairway to their room and then stops for moment before walking out the door of the hotel.

Next thing Charles knows, Mary arrives to see him. She tells him, "I remember that time you went away with Mr. Edwards. You were gone so long, and we all missed you so. I'll never forget what you told us when you went away. You said that no matter how hard it was being away, as long as we held each other in our hearts, it wouldn't be like we were really apart. We'd have our love, and we could hold it inside us, like we were really holding each other. Pa, you've always done what you felt what right for us, but there comes a time when you have to do what's right for *you*. I'm not a child anymore, Pa. I'm a woman. I've got my own life, and I'm gonna be happy. I'm a teacher, Pa. I'm doing what I love, and that's why I'm all right here. But not you, Pa. Not you. I can't be happy knowing you're staying here because of me. That's not fair to either one of us . . . I'll hold you I my heart, Pa."

Here is the child telling her father to be honest with himself; to be true and fair to himself. There are certain times when it isn't selfish to do what's best for ourselves. Sometimes it involves taking a risk, no matter how big and frightening that risk may be. I have a friend who, in her forties, found herself in a failed marriage and at a standstill, career-wise. She had an interest in buying a franchise of a successful company, but she was nervous. Scared. What if she couldn't do it? What if she worked hard, but the business didn't take off? She kept hesitating. Then one night, her twelve-year-old daughter said to her, "Mom, if you don't try something just because you're afraid, you can never accomplish anything." Twelve years old. Eye-opening and inspiring!

We all need that little reminder sometimes to be honest with ourselves, and that big push sometimes to go for it! Our children will benefit so much from this guidance. And once in a while, when it's our kids who light a fire under us and tell us to get moving, we will benefit, too.

The very worst thing you can do to a man is make him think he's a coward.
—Michael Landon

Chapter 12
Letting Our Children Go

"Well, You Can't Keep Your Children with You Forever ..."

In that scene where Mary tells Charles to look inside himself and realize that he has to be true to himself and leave Winoka, she's also saying that it's time for him to let her go. She's all grown up. Letting our children go is one of the most difficult parts of parenting. It isn't even something we have to dread as we look ahead to their adulthood, because letting go is a necessity throughout *all* the years of raising our kids. We let go when we send them to preschool. We let go (literally!) when we teach them to ride a two-wheeler. We let go when they drive away on the day they get their licenses. And eventually, we let go when they leave home. *That* one's a doozy!

Prairie parents, like us, deal with "all the feels" over the years as they learn to let their children go. The father of the little handicapped girl in "Town Party, Country Party" wants to keep his daughter home all the time so that she won't be hurt by the exclusion and teasing of others. He has to learn that his little girl can only grow if he allows her to venture out of the cocoon he's created for her.

Similarly, it's important for us to remember that our children have their own interests and dreams. What we want for them isn't always what *they* want. "Isaiah Edwards" has to come to terms with this in the episode "I'll Ride the Wind" (season three). His adopted son, "John," loves to read, write, and use his imagination. He wonders about nature. "Just studying that hawk up there," he tells Isaiah as they're loading hay onto a wagon. "What do you suppose is going on in his head? What's he thinking? He's got a brain like we have. What do you think is going on in his head while he's looking down at us pitching hay?"

Isaiah finds this strange and just shakes his head. "Sometimes I wonder about you, boy. You're riding the wind, and me, I'm just ridin' a hay wagon." He wants his son to become a farmer like him.

John is ecstatic when a magazine is interested in the poems he's written. He tells his parents that he plans to make a living as a writer and has asked Mary to marry him.

Isaiah doesn't get it at all. He's even more puzzled (and resentful) when John is awarded a four-year scholarship to college. "We're different, Boy," he says. "You and me, we're different. It's like we live on two different hills with a big ditch in between us. I mean, you're doing things, and I ain't got the faintest notion what they are."

Wanting to make Isaiah happy, John decides not to go to college. Before long, however, he has second thoughts about his decision. He doesn't admit it, but Mary knows.

"He's doing it for me and for you; not for himself," she says to Isaiah. He isn't a farmer. He was born for books and words and the music he can make with them. And we're taking them away from him. He'll stay if we ask him to, with the life gone out of him. And the music. I want him, more than you do maybe. But not that way. I don't think you do either."

Mary encourages John to head to college. She also convinces Isaiah to embrace the differences between himself and his son; to let him go find happiness doing what he loves. It isn't easy when our ideas about what is best for our children don't match their ideas. But they have to live their own lives and find their way

in this world, hopefully doing what they love and being who they truly are.

*****

A humorous episode called "Men will Be Boys" (season five) deals with Albert and Andy wanting to make their own way in the world and be treated like men. They've been working together for a man in town, and they're ready to drop out of school to work full time. Charles and Jonathan don't think they're old enough yet. The two fathers try to explain to the boys that the opportunity for an education is too important to pass up. When Albert and Andy aren't buyin' it, Charles and Jonathan come up with a scheme to teach the boys a lesson by sending them on an adventure by themselves.

Albert and Andy walk to Sleepy Eye through the woods and are supposed to pick up a letter at the post office there. Charles and Jonathan tell them that if they can make it to the city, get the letter, and bring it back to Walnut Grove, they can quit school and work full time. What the boys don't know is that Charles and Jonathan don't think they can do it and are following them the whole way (to make sure they stay safe). *This part of the story makes the episode funny, because the two men run into all kinds of trouble – and hunger – trying to keep up with the boys.*

It's a tough trip for Albert and Andy too, and in the end, even though they make it back to Walnut Grove, they've lost the letter and have been scared many times along the way. They decide they'd rather remain "boys" for a bit longer and not be in such a hurry to grow up.

This episode offers a nice balance between challenging kids to take responsibility while encouraging them to realize that they're still too young for certain things. Of course it also addresses the struggle we face as parents when our children are ready to grow up before we are ready to let them. I guess we have to try to meet them half way; allowing them certain freedoms and privileges while still keeping hold of the reigns.

Patrick Labyorteaux (who played Andy and was the brother of Matthew Labyorteaux, who played Albert) told me that he remembers "Men Will Be Boys" as his favorite episode. "My brother and I were both on the show. We got to go up into Northern California and hang out and just play in the woods. We were acting with each other . . . and the whole episode was just he and I and our dads on the show. And it was just the most fun! We had the best time!"

*****

The idea of letting go is repeated in "Back to School," the first episode of season six, and the famous one where Laura first lays eyes on Almanzo. It's love at first sight, and in her googly-eyed stupor, she accidentally calls him "Manly" instead of "Manny." He's a good sport about it, and tells her that now only *she* can call him Manly. In return, he comes up with a nickname for her; because her middle name is Elizabeth, he decides on "Beth." Laura is pumped that her crush is addressing her with this lovely, very grown-up name.

Consequently, she asks her pa to stop calling her "Half-Pint" in public. Laura wants to be considered a woman. She decides to work toward graduating from school and becoming a teacher. Charles and Caroline aren't sure she's quite ready for this, and Charles definitely isn't ready for her to be grown up. Luckily for him, Laura doesn't pass her graduation exam and has to stay in school. Charlie dodged *that* bullet and was able to hold onto his little girl for a while longer.

It isn't until months later, when Laura is offered a teaching position in a nearby town, that Charles has to start worrying. This episode is "Sweet Sixteen" (season six), a big one, because Almanzo finally starts to see Laura in a romantic way. Agreeing to drive her to and from her job at the beginning and end of each week, he notices how grown up Laura has become. Charles is far from overjoyed, especially when Almanzo asks Laura to go with him to the church social. *Geez, compared to what parents today have to worry about, I'd settle for the church social anytime!*

After months and months of hearing Laura gush about Manly, Charles finally begins to accept the fact that this dude is sticking around. He picks

Laura up from work on her birthday and hints to her during their ride home that Almanzo is most likely in love with her.

At the social, Charles looks at Laura and Almanzo on the dance floor and says to Caroline, "I have a terrible feeling I'm about to lose a daughter."

*****

"Losing her" isn't as easy as it sounds. "He Loves Me, He Loves Me Not" (season six) begins with Almanzo proposing to Laura. Charles, still not wanting to let Laura go quite yet, tells him that Laura can't get married until she's eighteen. *This has always been funny to me, because he was ready to let Mary marry John at the age of fifteen. I guess Pa becomes more protective as the years roll on.*

Almanzo is not at all jazzed about waiting two years to marry Laura. When he asks her to go against Charles' wishes and elope, she declines, and he leaves town. *Pigheaded!* A lot of drama pours out from there, but eventually the two wind up together, and Charles announces that they only have to wait *one* year to get married. *Baby steps.*

The side story in this script involves the entrance of "Percival Dalton" as a culinary business coach for Nellie. His efforts to train her are at first met with Nellie's bitchy defiance. She wants nothing to do with him or the hotel / restaurant her mother has built for her as a means of helping her find a husband. There is a comical scene here in which we witness Nellie's opposition and feel Percival's pain:

Percival (separating an egg): **"There. Now you try."** *Nellie just glares at him.* **"Miss Oleson,**

you're not gonna learn if you don't try. Now, please, go ahead." *Nellie picks up two eggs and slams them together.* **"You know, your father is paying me a lot of money to teach you. The least you could do is make an attempt."**

Nellie: "I didn't *ask* to be taught. I didn't *ask* for this restaurant . . . And you're *SHORT*."

Percival: "Shall we try again?"

Nellie: "Why don't you make a *short* cake? How 'bout some *short* ribs? Do we need any *short*ening? Ya know, you really oughta write a book: *Shortcuts to Cooking*!"

Percival: "Would you like to try again?!?!!"

Nellie: "That only took you a *short* time!"

Percival: "Would you like to try again?!?!!"

Nellie: "No I wouldn't! I wouldn't *like to try again*! I hate this place, and I hate cooking, and I hate short people! My mother gave me this place so I could get a husband. Did ya know that? Well I don't *want* a husband, and I don't *want* this place, and I don't *want* to learn how to separate eggs!" *(She smashes all the eggs into the bowl.)* **"There, Quasimodo! I'm all done!"**

Percival: *(picking up the bowl and dumping the whole thing over her head)* **"I also have a very *short* temper! Why your mother ever built this place for you, I'll never know! You certainly can't cook, and you certainly have no right to be dealing with the public! And as pretty as you are, you don't need a restaurant to catch a husband in the first place!"**

That's all it takes. Percival thinks she's pretty. Nellie's in love. From here on out, she commits to learning how to cook and run her business. She also tries to find ways to make him interested in her, despite their height difference. Eventually she knows, with Nels' prompting, that she needs to just tell Percival she loves him. When he reciprocates, they decide immediately to get married. Another side-splitting scene:

Nellie: (interrupting his ballgame with the kids in town) **"Percival?"**

Percival: (getting hit in the head with the ball) **"What?"**

Nellie: "I have something to tell you . . . I love you. I LOVE you."

Percival: "I don't know what to say."

Nellie: "Well . . . Do you?"

Percival: "Yes. I love you, too . . . But, what about, uh . . . I'm not getting any taller."

Nellie: (giggling) **"And I'm not getting any shorter!"**

Percival: "Will you marry me?"

Nellie: "Yes. Oh, yes!"

The happy couple proceeds to make out on Main Street, Walnut Grove, USA. Nels and Harriet open the window of their bedroom and peak out. Harriet is appalled at the kissing!

Harriet: (Gasp!) **"What are you two doing?!?! In the middle of the street?!!"**

Nellie: We're getting married, Mother! We're getting married!"

Percival: "Tomorrow!"

Harriet: "Tomorrow! You can't! Well, there's no gown, and a church wedding?!?!"

Percival: "Oh, we can't have a church wedding, Mrs. Oleson. Uh ... Something simple; outside!"

Harriet: "No church wedding??? Why not????"

Percival: "I'm Jewish."

Harriet: "Oh, he's JEWISH?!?!?!?!!!!!!" She screams . . . *Some bigotry never goes away!*

Nels: *(trying to save Harriet from having a coronary)* **"Now, calm down. Calm down. He's marrying our daughter."**

Harriet: *(taking a second, third, fourth look)* **"Awww, they *are* kind of a cute couple, aren't they? Oh . . . I suppose it's no worse than being *short.* Oh, Nels, my little girl."**

When I wanted to include this scene in this book, I recorded it on my phone so I could play it back and type the dialogue out. Almost as funny as the scene itself was the sound of my laughter in the background of my recording; a true testament to the brilliance of the writing and acting! Richard Bull and Katherine MacGregor brought a comedy to Little House that was not only genius but a valuable balance to the often sobering storylines. The Oleson family added such an important layer to the show through the years.

This side story is an example of parents needing to accept a person of another religion as their child's choice for a life partner. Mrs. Oleson, for a change, takes a surprisingly level-headed approach to Nellie's decision. Smart move! Once our children are grown, they have to be free to mark their own trails.

*****

Both the Ingalls and the Olesons have to let go and say goodbye to their children in "The Reincarnation of Nellie" (season seven). The show opens with Harriet bitching to Caroline about how Nellie and her family have been in New York visiting her in-laws for four weeks. Nels comes in with the news that Nellie's father-in-law has passed away. Harriet is devastated when she learns that Nellie and her family are staying in New York permanently. Caroline expresses her empathy, and Nels says, "Well, you can't keep your children with you forever. It's just that New York is *so* far."

That evening, Mary and Adam have similar news.

"Charles, I've been in Walnut Grove almost six months now," says Adam *(who has now regained his sight and is a lawyer),"* and in that time I've had exactly five cases. Aside from the first one involving Mr. Mills and the land-swindling, my most exciting case was Morgan versus Swenson, concerning the theft of an outhouse. I just can't make a living here. So, last week, I contacted my father's old law firm, and they told me that they have an opening."

Silence.

Saying goodbye is tough. "Don't let those city people go changing you too much," Charles says to Mary.

"I won't," she assures him. "I'll eat with my shoes off at least once a week."

"I love you."

"I love you, too."

Caroline tells her, "I won't cry, and I won't say goodbye."

Knowing what's best for their children, they accept Mary and Adam's decision. It isn't easy, but their only choice is to let them go. Part of our success as parents is raising our children in a way that gives them courage and confidence to leave our nest and fly on their own.

*****

Sarah Carter's high and mighty father has a terrible time accepting his daughter as an independent woman in season nine's "Sins of the Fathers." The Carters have moved into the Ingalls' old house and are loving their life in Walnut Grove when Sarah's father, "Elliott," arrives unexpectedly from New York. Showering the family with gifts, he avoids telling Sarah that her mother has passed away. When he does share the news with her, he twists the truth, saying that her mother died quickly one day from influenza.

Upon visiting Sarah's newspaper office in town, Elliott begins to criticize it (and Sarah) almost immediately. "Well now, why don't you give me a grand tour of the Walnut Grove Gazette?"

Sarah chuckles nervously. "I'm afraid you're looking at it. This is the sum and total of my publishing empire."

"Then I'm surprised that you have any empire at all," Elliott says. "If you want to publish a newspaper, you might as well publish it right. Now, what were you working on when I walked in here?"

"Uh, just an article about the school book drive. Do you wanna read it?"

"No, and I don't think many of your readers want to read it, either." Elliott sits down at the desk and takes over. "I'm going to show you how a real newspaper publisher works!"

Next, he pays a visit to John at his blacksmith shop, criticizing his work as well and offering him a job in New York. "I want a better life for Sarah and the boys. As far as I can see, you're the only one holding them back."

As the days pass, Elliott continues to dominate Sarah's work, even printing a gossip column written by the town crier, Harriet. Its content destroys the reputation of a woman in town.

Sarah confides in Laura. "I don't know why I let that man do this to me. I feel like such a child when I'm around him."

"Well, if it's any help to you, I feel exactly the same way when I'm around my father. My ma told me that we probably never really get over that. It took me years to convince my pa that Almanzo and I should get married," Laura confides. "Even after he said yes, I could tell that deep down inside, he wasn't ready to let go of me yet."

"I'm afraid he's gonna resent John until the day he dies," Sarah says.

At their house, Elliott continues to insult Sarah and John. "This shack you call a home isn't fit for human habitation. The boys sleep in a loft; you pump water from a well by hand . . . I'm glad I didn't let Emma *(Sarah's mother)* come out here after all."

Sarah sits up. "Mama wanted to come visit us? Why didn't you say something about this before?"

"I didn't think it was important," Elliott says.

"You deliberately kept me from her at a time when she needed me most?" Sarah protests. You had no right to do that."

"I had every right. I'm your father."

"Well you're everybody's father, aren't you? Mama's, mine, John's, everybody's! Everybody has to do what you say!"

"Is that the kind of nonsense life in this prairie town has taught you?"

"It's taught me independence! It's taught me that I'm not your little girl anymore! I'm a grown woman with a husband and two children. You may get your way with your editors and your reporters, and even the president of the United States. But not with me. Not ever again!"

Elliott leaves, and Sarah feels relieved that she's spoken her mind and stood up to him.

The next day, however, she has regrets. What if they never see each other again? The Carters decide to go into town and say goodbye before the stage coach leaves.

"I know you want what's best for us," Sarah says to her father, "but I-"

"No," Elliott interrupts. "I don't want it for you, but for myself. When you get older, you find out that you're not as strong and independent as you think you are. You look around and suddenly find you're all alone. The top floor of The Globe Telegram gets to be a mighty lonely place at times. John, I wish you the very best. To be honest with you, the only hurt you did me was to take my place."

Sarah and Elliott exchange somewhat formal goodbyes, and then Sarah calls out to him. "Daddy!" Running into his arms, she says, "I love you."

The tearful man boards the stage and reaches his hand out the window, saying, "I love you, too."

Pamela Roylance ("Sarah") loves this episode. She shared with me that she feels it sends the important message to patch up your differences with others before it's too late.

Oh my gosh! I'm not sobbing. YOU'RE sobbing!! This ending is a killer!! I cry each time. This is such a true depiction of a parent who never really wanted to let go of his little girl, even though she's happy and successful in her adult life. He realizes at the end that he has been self-centered and foolish, putting his own happiness before his daughter's. His need for his family to be in New York isn't for their well-being, but for his own. It takes a lot of courage for Elliott to admit this, and a lot of "letting go," too. As parents, we have a responsibility to love, respect, teach, and take care of our children while they are with us. We also have a responsibility to give our children wings and let from fly out of our arms when they are grown and ready. We've done a good job. Now it's time to reap the rewards of our hard work by watching them go do great things! Those things may not be what we would choose for them, but that choice isn't ours. We have to let go and let them live.

*****

One last example of this separation struggle exists in the episode "May I Have This Dance?" (season nine). Willie Oleson is graduating from school *(I know, right?!?!)*, and he has fallen in love with his classmate, "Rachel Brown." His mother, of course, has grandiose ideas for his future. She has arranged for him to take the examination for entry to "the university." What she doesn't know is that Willie has no desire or plans to go to college. He has asked Rachel to marry him, and he wants to stay in Walnut Grove and run the family restaurant.

Because he knows that Harriet will not "take kindly" to his plan, Willie decides that his only choice is to fail the exam on purpose, so that he doesn't have to go away to school.

Willie is right. When he receives his exam results, Harriet is appalled. "How on Earth do you expect to get into the university if you can't pass the entrance exam?!" She rants and whines, devising a plan to get a tutor and have Willie retake the test. *She really is the ultimate helicopter mom.*

Willie speaks up. "I don't expect to get into the university! I expect to stay here and run the restaurant! "Mother, I failed the exam *on purpose*!" he yells. "I'm *not* gonna take it again!

I'm gonna stay in Walnut Grove, and I'm gonna run the restaurant, and I'm gonna marry Rachel Brown!"

Harriet and Nels are both stunned. Harriet collapses dramatically into a chair. Nels follows Willie out of the room and proceeds to support his decision and compliment his choice of a bride. *I love Nels!*

Willie is over the moon when he asks Rachel's father for her hand and is granted permission. Nels congratulates him, but Harriet? Big snub. She refuses to talk to Willie about his plans but carries on about them to everyone in town.

Willie gets fed up with Harriet's 'tude and goes thundering into the mercantile with Rachel. "Mother? I have something to say to you. And I'm only gonna say it once, so I want you to *pay attention!*"

"Willie, there's nothing that you haven't said-" Harriet starts in.

"Mother! I'm talking! You're listening! You've been complaining to me, and to Father, and to anyone else in Walnut Grove who'll listen to you that Rachel is ruining my life. Now, I've kept quiet about it, because I thought you'd realize how wrong you are. But I'm *not* going to keep quiet about it any longer. If anyone is ruining my chances for a happy life around here, *you* are!"

"*Me?!*" Harriet shrieks.

"Yes, you! Rachel is my *best* chance for a happy life, and I don't *ever* wanna hear you say another unkind word about her! Now, we are going to go open up the restaurant. And you can just stay here until you accept the fact that Rachel and I are getting married! Because that's exactly what we're gonna do!"

"Fine! Fine!" Harriet shouts. "Go ahead! Marry her! I don't care! I won't be there! I promise you that!"

"Fine!" Willie shouts back. "That's *your* decision!" He and Rachel turn to leave. Willie stops and turns back for a moment. "Oh, by the way . . . Mr. Edwards is going to be my best man!" *Bwa ha ha ha! Harriet is roasted. She can't stand Mr. Edwards.*

On the morning of the wedding, Harriet sits in the back of the church, dressed fully in black, face covering and all, as if she's attending a funeral. The looks on various people's faces are priceless as Harriet's sobs are heard throughout the church.

"Glad you could make it to the wedding, Harriet," Nels says to her when the ceremony ends. Later he has more choice words for her. "Brings back memories, doesn't it? Remember how upset my mother was? She didn't want me to quit college to get married. I believe she said that it would ruin my life."

Harriet's expression tells us that's she's forgotten this part of their past. Nels reminds her that, like Willie, he didn't care what his mother thought. He was an adult, making adult decisions, and it was time for his mother to step aside; just as it is time for Harriet to get out of Willie's way and let him go.

Let's face it – letting our children go is just plain hard. Whether it's allowing them to walk into town with their friends during the elementary school years, getting them an iPhone with scary apps during their middle school days, giving them the keys to our car when they're in high school, or simply allowing them to return to school during a global pandemic (!!!), letting them go and grow on their own is difficult. It's frightening; but if we trust in ourselves and all the things we have taught our children, and if we believe that they will take those things we've instilled and apply them on their own, we'll be okay. And so will they.

"I think all of us create our own miracles."
—Michael Landon

Chapter 13
Favorite Quotes, Ideas, and Memories from "Little House"

"As Long as You Do Your Best, Laura, We'll Always Be Proud of You."

In each and every episode of *Little House on the Prairie*, there are takeaways; thoughts that stay with me and make me reflect on life. Some are happy, some are sad. Some are beautiful, some are dark. Some are hilarious! But *each* of them teaches a lesson, makes me chuckle, or at least gives me "all the feels!" Here are may faves from each episode:

"We're home."
Charles to Caroline and the girls when they settle in Walnut Grove. ("A Harvest of Friends")

"Her smile is the last thing I see before I close my eyes at night and the first thing I *wanna* see in the morning."
Laura reading her essay at school on Parents' Day. *Tear-jerker!*

("Country Girls")

Whenever I wake my children up, I make sure I have a warm smile on my face, because I've always remembered this quote.

"I visit with you each day in my thoughts."

Charles in his letter home while he's away working.

("100 Mile Walk")

"Mr. Edwards! I can spit as far as you now! I've been practicing!"

Laura when Charles brings Mr. Edwards to Walnut Grove. *Spitting ability is a big sense of pride for Laura!*

("Mr. Edwards Homecoming")

"Nothing is solved by shutting off the other person's argument."

Caroline to Laura and Mary when they are arguing about a boy.

Sound advice from Ma. She always knew just how to handle things. I'm always reminding my children to hear each other out, and to keep their unkind thoughts and words to themselves.

Also from this episode, the iconic Little House expression:

"Don't mind if I do!"

Johnny when Laura asks him if he'd like to go on a picnic.

("The Love of Johnny Johnson")

"We oughta have our funerals while we're still alive, so we can say goodbye to everybody."

Laura during the funeral of a neighbor.

("If I Wake Die Before I Die")

This title is brilliant, too!

"Nellie's poor. She has no happiness inside."

Olga, understanding that money can't buy happiness.

("Town Party, Country Party")

"I don't think I want hair on my chest!"

Laura, gagging down a chunk of Mr. Edwards' rattlesnake stew, which he says will put hair on her chest.

("Ma's Holiday")

"You needn't tell your father about this."

Caroline, after smacking a baseball out of the schoolyard while trying to prove a point to her students.

("School Mom")

Of course, the girls told Pa!

"Do they have one for eleven cents?"

Mary trying to buy a new, glass doll head after Laura's is accidentally broken.

("The Raccoon")

They cost $1.20!

"The next thing you know, she's gonna be changing the name of this town to Olesonville!"

Mr. Kennedy's reaction when Harriet offers to donate a church bell with a plaque dedicating it in the Olesons' name.

("The Voice of Tinker Jones")

Olesonville doesn't come to fruition in this particular episode, but check out Season 9!

"If you forget this punishment, all your girls could to expect you to forget the next one, and the next one after that."

Reverend Alden, counseling Caroline after she's punished Mary.

("The Award")

This is solid advice. Follow-through is KEY!

"The closer you are to God, the more likely He is to listen."

Reverend Alden, when Laura asks him what God can do and how she can be sure He'll hear her prayers.

("The Lord is My Shepherd")

Unfortunately, Laura is a little girl and takes him very literally. She runs away to the top of a faraway mountain to pray!

"Santa Claus comes down the chimney. If he comes down the chimney, he'll get all burned up!"

Carrie, fearing for Santa Claus' life on Christmas Eve.

("Christmas at Plum Creek")

Luckily, Charles finds her standing by the fireplace and explains that Santa is magic and won't feel a thing. This is such a sweet scene.

"Please, just tell me about it one more time. She took the whole basket of eggs and just dumped it right on his head, and then he paid you for them?"

Charles laughing hysterically after Caroline describes a fight she witnessed between Harriet and Nels.

("Family Quarrel")

Michael Landon's fantastic laugh was contagious!

"Twenty years from now, she'll still be a young woman. And I . . . Ya know something? I don't care. I really don't care. For the first time in my life, I really feel alive."

Dr. Baker, aware that he's way too old to marry Kate but trying to pretend it'll be okay.

("Doctor's Lady")

In the end, he does the right thing and lets her go, but this a sad one to watch.

"The roads were lonely. I guess that's why I gave some of them the magic powders; to have them feel beholden to me. To think that I was a little better, a little taller, and I little wiser than I really am."

"Mr. O'Hara," a magician who comes to Walnut Grove and convinces the townspeople that he can cure them with his special powder "remedy." He eventually has to be honest with Laura – and everyone – and admit that he's a phony.

("Circus Man")

The continuity in this scene is way off. First Laura's braids are both in the front. Then one is in back. Then both are in front front again. Then the other braid is in back. I guess when you've watched these episodes as many times as I have, you start to notice these things. Seriously, though, continuity must be one of the more challenging parts of filming!

"Sometimes it's difficult to understand why God allows things like this to happen. When it's all over, instead of being weakened by it, we find we're made stronger."

Reverend Alden, after an outbreak of typhus in Walnut Grove is finally cured.

("Plague")

There's a scene in this episode where Charles comes home for a few minutes (he's been exposed to the illness, so he's stayed in town to help Dr. Baker take care of the ill). Charles stays on the wagon when Caroline and the girls come out to see him. He asks Laura for some "salt risin' bread," and when she brings it out to him, she sets it down on a napkin on the ground. No hugs, no kisses, no contact. This reminds me of the quarantine we've been in during the Covid pandemic and the six-foot social distancing we've had to maintain.

On lighter note, there's second quote I love from this episode. Laura tells her parents that she has a toothache. The family talks about how much candy Nellie and Willie are always eating, and Charles assures everyone that their teeth will soon be rotten.

Mary: "I told Nellie her teeth would fall out, but she didn't care. She'll just *buy* teeth, like her mother has."

Caroline: "I didn't know Mrs. Oleson has store-boughten teeth."

Charles: "How could you tell? She never smiles!"

I guess we all know a "Mrs. Oleson."

"Well, you're just in time. That's my hold-out bottle. This is the one I didn't tell you about. I thought is was time that I found something out, and I did; it gave me some pleasure to pour it out."

John Stewart, an alcoholic whom Charles helps with his recovery. Charles finds him in the barn one night, pouring out the last of his whiskey.

("Child of Pain")

This episode's depiction of both alcoholism and child abuse is so well done. And this moment makes me so happy for the character every time I watch it.

"Not one of your friends or neighbors is going to plant a seed 'til they've plowed and planted *your* field."

Charles to Joe Colter, after he's been injured in an accident while on the road buying corn seed for the men of the town. When the accident delays his return to Walnut Grove, the men suspect that he's taken off with their money with no plan of returning. They are unkind to Joe's pregnant wife, and when Joe finally gets home and finds out, he and his wife decide to move away. In order to make up for their awful behavior, the men get to work on the Colters' farm, planting their crop for them.

("Money Crop")

"You have my permission to argue if it'll help keep you warm."

Caroline to her girls, who are playing hopscotch on the floor of an old cabin where the Ingalls have taken shelter during a blizzard.

("Survival")

I've always loved this line! My kids, however, are fortunate enough to never really know what it truly feels like to be freezing. Lucky children.

Mr. Edwards: School's important. It's real, real important!"

Johnny Johnson: "Well now there was this boy in Illinois, who only had one year of schoolin' and five different teachers before he started learning on his own."

Mr. Edwards: "He probably turned out to be a fiddle-footed ignoramus!"

Johnny: "He turned out to be President Lincoln."

Mr. Edwards: "Oh."

Mr. Edwards trying to talk Johnny Johnson out of quitting school.

("To See the World")

"Winning isn't everything. The important thing is competing and doing your best."

Charles telling the girls about sportsmanship before the town's big day of competitions, celebrating the anniversary of Walnut Grove.

("Founder's Day")

I wish more parents today would share this philosophy when it comes to their children's athletics. But I digress …

"What a family. It does make a man proud … I couldn't do it without you!"

Charles, when Caroline and the girls want to work and help him earn the money he owes to the mercantile.

("The Richest Man in Walnut Grove")

"I kinda thought it was something like that. That old saying isn't true is it, about sticks and stones? Names *do* hurt."

Charles when Mary admits that she'd hidden her glasses, and lied about losing them, because Nellie was teasing her.

("Four Eyes")

I've always loved the way Charles handles the news when Mary first tells him she's lost the glasses, as well as the way he reacts to her admission about lying. He is disappointed but stays calm. He also empathizes with her, recognizing that it's hard to ignore name-calling. I've never understood why that "sticks and stones" saying is so popular. Names and teasing can be just as painful as a punch in the gut. Sometimes even more so.

"Half Pint, the more you love, the more you hurt."

Charles explaining to Laura why the old man she's trying to befriend keeps shutting her out. The man has lost his wife and seems unable to move on without her. Laura tells him, **"Just have faith. That's what my pa says. And then we'll see our loved ones when we get there."**

("Haunted House")

Perfect.

"Well, it gets you outdoors, and, no one could argue, it's good, healthy exercise."

Caroline talking about baseball after Walnut Grove's big game against Sleepy Eye.

("In the Big Inning")

Good, healthy exercise . . . a refreshing idea with all of the screen time our kids have these days!

"What are you gonna tell Mary and Laura? You told them they could get along with *anybody* for *two short days*!"

Caroline challenging Charles after he finds out that Harriet has decided to come along on the campout the Ingalls have invited Nels, Nellie, and Willie to join them for. When Harriet announces she's coming, Charles announces he's *not*!

("The Campout")

This is an example of how, as parents, we have to practice what we preach.

"Swallowing your pride doesn't give you indigestion … And you'll be no worse off than you are now."

Caroline explaining to Laura and Grace that sometimes we have to stop waiting for others and just take the bull by the horns and try to make things happen ourselves.

("The Spring Dance")

"That's the way you live this life. Each day, one at a time. Now if you spend your life worrying about something that's gonna happen, before you know it, your life's over and you've spent an awful lot of it just worrying. Hey, ya hear that *(laughter)*? That's what life's all about. Laughin' and lovin' each other … and knowing that people aren't really gone when they die. We have all the good memories to sustain us until we see them again."

Charles comforting Laura after she finds out that their neighbor, who has three children, is going to die.

("Remember Me")

This is such a beautiful scene, and an incredibly special message about love during loss. I remember reading an article about in People Magazine *that was written when Melissa Gilbert was a teenager and still starring in* Little House. *She said something to the effect of, "I try to live every day for that day." Sounds like she learned a lot from her amazing friend and mentor, Michael Landon. There's also a quote from this episode (which I'll share later) that Melissa Gilbert read at Michael Landon's funeral. Clearly, there are messages that really apply to our real lives when we experience the loss of a loved one.*

"Some folks just like to think the worst of other folks. Maybe he's just afraid of being hurt. If you never love someone, you never have to worry about that person hurting you. Friends and loved ones are always the ones to give you joy and sorrow. That's why you can't go through this life being afraid to love. 'Cause without love, there just isn't any reason for living."

Charles comforting Laura *(he does that a lot, doesn't he???)* after she has befriended a new neighbor and he is too guarded to let her in.

("Ebenezer Sprague")

"A promise is a promise. It's yours."

Laura to her friend, Jonah, after she's told him she'll give him her fishing pole when they collect all the money from the "gold" they've found. Even after realizing that they haven't struck it rich, she still gives Jonah the pole.

("At the End of the Rainbow")

A girl of her word. It's so important to keep promises, even when things don't turn out as we may have planned.

"What do you *MEAN* you *gave* it to her?!?!"

Mary when Laura can't sell a "sickly" old woman the medicine they've ordered, so she kind of "donates" it.

("The Gift")

This is actually a funny scene. As a viewer, you kind of want to commend Laura for helping another person out. What she doesn't know is that the person is playing her, too. She's not sickly at all; just likes the alcohol in the "remedy!"

"He can't read. Isaiah can't read, and he can't write. You wanted him to be proud of you, and he feels the same way. That's why he didn't want you to know he can't read. 'Cause he wants you to respect him."

Charles telling John that his pa didn't really blow off the letter John has written to him about his feelings. He can't read it.

("His Father's Son")

Radames Pera, who played John, told me he loved this episode, because he "got to work with Victor a lot, and Michael directed . . . . That was a pinnacle experience for me on the show."

"I did it, Miss Beadle. And I'm not sorry, because it's the truth."

"Jason," admitting that he wrote "Jason Loves Laura" in a heart on the classroom blackboard, after everyone (especially Nellie) has been teasing Laura about her crush on him.

("The Talking Machine")

Put that in your lunch pail and eat it, Nellie!

"All you can do is your best."

Caroline telling Mary to just try her best on an important exam competition.

("The Pride of Walnut Grove")

"Everybody likes to have a day all to herself once in a while; just to think and relax."

Caroline looking forward to a day of baking while Charles and the girls go camping.

("A Matter of Faith")

Little does she know that an infection in her leg will make her fight for her life while she's home alone. This is a "different" kind of Little House episode with a different feel, and even some different camera angles. Kind of a nail-biter, too! Karen Grassle is terrific in this one.

"But Mr. Edwards is letting *Carl* go." . . . . "But our pa's letting *us* go."

Laura playing both Charles and Isaiah, hoping that each will agree to let the Mary, Carl, and her go on a trip with them.

("The Runaway Caboose")

Don't we love it when our kids try to pull this?

"You owe my wife a thank you. She asked me to be nice to you."

Charles, when he's completely disgusted with the control-freak teacher who has taken Miss Beadle's place and is mistreating Laura and the rest of the class.

("Troublemaker")

Sometimes, when people are despicable, it's reeeeaaalllllly hard to be nice, isn't it? This is one of many times when Caroline reminds Charles to keep his cool. Sometimes he manages to do so, and sometimes he caves.

"He booted me out, too. He found out I was Irish!"

"Murphy," a work partner of Charles and his friends, who has been prejudiced against the one black man on their team. When the men try to ride the train home, the conductor won't allow the black man inside the train car. He is sent out to the freight car, and Charles, Isaiah, and eventually Murphy, join him. Murphy makes this joke, because the other men are shocked when he comes out to the freight car to sit with them.

("The Long Road Home")

Victor French 's (Isaiah) laughing is hilarious here.

"Caroline, you're gonna get your dishes!"

Charles (saying this to himself) is so excited to be earning the money for a set of china dishes he knows Caroline will love. She hasn't asked for them; he just wants to do something to surprise her make her happy.

("For My Lady")

So fun, and so romantic!

"You be happy you live here; this fine country. You have freedoms here; worship, meetings, speech, press. Do you know how much this freedom means? In my prayers, I give thanks that my family and I could come live here – the home of the freedoms – the United States of America. The best country in the whole world. "

"Yuli Pyatakov," a Russian immigrant, who is honored to live in America, even though his struggle to pay his taxes has cost him his land and home.

("Centennial")

I enjoy this quote, because I am a very proud American and am always grateful to have been born here. Despite some of the difficulties our country is facing, it is still the greatest country in the world. What a privilege it is to be an American!

"Everyone is afraid sometimes. The only way to stop running from your shame is to face it. There's no shame in the truth."

"Mrs. Whipple," comforting her morphine-addicted son, who can't live with himself after running from danger during the war and losing his friend.

("Soldier's Return")

I like this quote because it applies to ***all*** *of us at one time or another. We all get scared. It's part of life. Yes, though, the truth can set us free.*

"Always give a stranger a chance, Child. Because if you don't, they'll remain a stranger."

"Mr. Simms," after Laura admits that she doesn't like him because he is buying the house she doesn't want to leave.

("Going Home")

"Ya know, you were really lucky havin' a dog love you like that. There are a lot of people who go through their whole life and never have anybody to love 'em. But you know, there's an end to everything. Even us ... What with God taking care of all those *(animals on Noah's ark)***, you can just be sure that He'll want a pretty little puppy like yours in Heaven."**

"Caleb Hodgekiss," consoling "Alicia Edwards" after her puppy dies.

("The Collection")

" 'Charlie's Fiddle?' How does he do it? How does he put into words exactly what I hear and feel when I hear your pa play?!"

Caroline to Mary, in amazement when reading one of John's poems.

("I'll Ride the Wind")

Charles' fiddle was a subtle yet important part of Little House. He would play joyful music during celebratory times and soothing songs in stressful moments.

The fiddle of the real Charles Ingalls is on display at the Rocky Ridge Farm in Mansfield, Missouri.

"An animal is no different than a person. It needs to be with someone who loves it. Take her home."

Nels giving Laura her horse back after Nellie has mistreated it and then lied about being crippled.

("Bunny")

Nellie & Willie: *(chanting)* **"Laura smells like a dirty horse! Laura smells like a dirty horse!"**

Nellie: "I'm glad my pa gave her back to you. She smells bad."

Laura: *(throwing a manure-filled rakeful of hay on them)* **"Don't we all?"**

Nellie trying to make it seem like she doesn't care that she lost her horse for being a bitch.

("The Race")

Laura: "He winked at me. You saw him!"

Carl: "He could've had something in his eye."

Laura: "If Mrs. Oleson is going to see her mother, she's gotta be on the morning stage."

Carl: "Of course she is."

Laura: "She *can't* be. She hasn't got a head!"

Laura attempting to convince Carl that she saw Nels chop of Harriet's head, and that Nels wants Laura to keep it a secret between him and her.

("The Monster of Walnut Grove")

"I have to listen to everybody. 'Have to go to school when I don't want to. Chores all the time. Mary always bossin' me around. Carrie just doin' as she pleases . . . . "

Laura explaining to her grandpa why she wants to run away from home.

("Journey in the Spring")

The things bothering her are pretty traditional for any kid, especially a middle child. I think everyone tries to run away at least once during his or her childhood.

When my son was about six, he packed his little suitcase one summer day, announced he was running away, and went out onto the back deck. He was out there for about twenty minutes, at which point he re-entered the house for an A/C break. Good stuff! Lucky for him, it wasn't 1879.

"That was a very fiery sermon the Reverend Alden gave this morning … I guess he changed his mind. He said he was gonna talk about, 'Love all creatures, great and small.' "

Caroline after church, not knowing that Reverend Alden was butted in the rear end by a billy goat the day before.

("Fred")

"And 'Bubba' *is* your given name?"

Miss Beadle welcoming a new student to school, despite the other students' giggles in reaction to his name.

("The Bully Boys")

This part actually makes me giggle, because the day after I gave birth to my daughter, my husband was greeted by two little girls in our neighborhood.

They congratulated him and asked what the baby's name was. Completely straight-faced, he answered, "I'm glad you asked, because we're having trouble deciding. We're either going to call her 'Colleen' or 'Bubba.' "

The girls (ages 8 and 10) tried to be polite and shared with him that they preferred "Colleen." Those two should have known from then on what kind of neighbors they were dealing with.

Now, nearly fourteen years later, my daughter says to me, "Mom. When you had a cringey name like 'Alicia,' how could you name me 'Colleen?' It sounds like I was born in the 1970s."

Hmph. She clearly doesn't enjoy her name **or** *mine. Imagine I had chosen something from the 1870s. I wonder what names were "cringey" then?*

"I'll never forget you for the rest of my life."

Laura saying goodbye to a blind man who helped her find her way through the woods and get to a doctor after Charles has been accidentally shot during a hunting accident.

("The Hunters")

After Laura and Charles leave, the man (played by Burl Ives!) says to his son, "We'd better get to work!" These are welcomed words to the son, who, up until this point, has watched his father sit around feeling sorry for himself because he can't see. Sometimes, once we've dealt with adversity, we find ourselves stronger!

"And the angels said unto them, 'Fear not. For behold, I bring you good tidings of great joy, which shall be to all people. For unto you is born this day in the city of David a savior, which is Christ the Lord."

Charles reading from the bible on Christmas morning after a terrible blizzard prevents Walnut Grove's children from finding their way home from school and takes the life of one of their neighbors.

("Blizzard")

"Loudy, you were right, and I was wrong . . . . It was because she married you. I loved her."

Lars Hanson, admitting after years of anger toward an alcoholic man that he'd always refused to hire him because the woman Lars loved had chosen to marry the other man.

("Little Girl Lost")

Caroline: "Why don't you get your buckets and go pick raspberries."

Mary: "Ya think it'll be all right?"

Caroline: "Well, there's no road up there. I don't think you'll see anyone."

Laura: "If we do, we'll run!"

Caroline: *(sighing)* **"You don't have to run. Just pick the berries and come on home. We'll have pie tonight."**

Caroline, trying to make the most of the situation when Scarlet Fever hits walnut Grove and the townspeople are quarantined.

("Quarantine")

This episode is so relatable right now, during this global pandemic. In fact, when I told Alison Arngrim ("Nellie") the title of this book, she made a reference to this episode and the episode "Plague," agreeing that history is repeating itself in a sense; and affirming that Little House continues to comfort people, especially during this difficult time.

Finding things to keep ourselves and our children upbeat and occupied has been a struggle for many. In the Little House days, there was no internet, so virtual learning wasn't an option. I don't know if that's a good thing or a bad thing. I'm kidding! Of course, we're lucky to have the technology we do today; but I have to admit, sometimes I'd rather be picking berries and eating pie with my kids than trying to figure out how to teach them this new-fangled way of doing math . . . and "screenshotting" (is that even a word???) on their chromebooks the work they did on loose-leaf so it can be sent electronically to their teachers. Seriously? About that pie . . . I'll take mine a la mode.

I love the end of the "Quarantine" episode. After Laura has discovered that she's covered with the red spots that are symptomatic of the fever, she goes to stay with Mr. Edwards and Alicia (who has the fever). When Dr. Baker is finally able to come examine her, he begins to chuckle. "You've got poison ivy, Honey!"

"Play acting's all right I guess. But when it turns out right, real life's a whole lot better."

Mary, when things have a happy ending in the life of a classmate with whom she and Laura performed in a school play.

("Little Women")

"You may as well know the truth about this. Those stories Papa's told about me being a captive aren't true. I married White Buffalo because I loved him. And Spotted Eagle is our son. Does that shock you? My husband left the reservation because we were starving. He left to try to find game;

food for his family! And the soldiers killed him for breaking their rules. And now I have to live the way Papa says, but it won't change the fact that I loved an Indian. Now if you'd rather not stay, I'll understand."

A new neighbor explaining over coffee her recent past to Caroline, who has come to welcome her to town. In true Caroline fashion, she is non-judgmental and responds, "I take cream and sugar."

("Injun Kid")

That Caroline is always a good friend.

Charles: "Mary, the doctor can't help you if you don't tell him everything. Have you had an upset stomach?

Mary: "A little, I guess."

Charles: "Well why didn't you say something?"

Mary: "I *can't stand* the taste of paregoric! Ma was sure to give me some! I'm sorry."

Dr. Baker: "Don't be. I hate the taste of paregoric!"

The start of Mary's stomach infection after she's kicked by one of their horses.

("To Live with Fear")

It's funny how kids will tell us they're sick when they want to avoid a test at school or something else unpleasant; and then they'll tell us they aren't *sick when they really are, just to avoid taking medicine (or missing out on something fun). Part of being a kid, I guess. I can remember, at age 7, sucking cool air into my mouth while my mother was taking my temperature, because I was supposed to perform in a play at school that day, and I didn't want to miss my big debut.*

"I remember when I could hear the women crying and singing …
'Death is the robber, but it can't steal me.
'Cause I've been called by the man from Galilee.
Lord, I never been up, and I'll never go down.
'Cause my soul is heaven bound!'

Solomon Henry recalling a poem/song that his people used to sing on the plantation.

("The Wisdom of Solomon")

Todd Bridges was terrific here. His emotion and delivery were completely convincing. His character was adorable and tragic all at the same time. He did some phenomenal work here. This episode is a real favorite of mine. Containing so very many important messages, it never gets old.

"I wouldn't be in your dumb old club for all the gumdrops in your father's store! Now leave us alone!

Laura telling Nellie off after she makes fun of Anna's stuttering.

("The Music Box")

All too often, our kids are pressured into making bad choices because someone else bribes them. Laura caves in the middle of this episode, but she stands her ground at the end (which is most important).

"We don't need them! We'll have a party of our own!"

Mary and Laura accepting their classmate, Elmer, and welcoming him to hang out with them after Nellie prevents the other kids from attending their party.

("The Election")

Charles: "We best keep that shot gun around."

Isaiah: "Yeah. 'Reckon I oughta load it too."

Charles and Isaiah after scaring off a couple of shady men who seemed to want a look at the gold they've found.

("Gold Country")

"You don't have to have walls and a roof to have hospitality … It's a feeling of being loved and needed … Hurting goes away, but love, never. Loving is the greatest gift the good Lord gave us. Don't waste it. Not for a moment."

Kezia Horn, explaining to Laura how she feels unwanted and unloved, just like the stray dog Laura keeps rejecting.

("Castoffs")

"There's only one thing in this world you can do better than anybody else. Be yourself . . . If you didn't feel a little bit of pain or sorrow, how would you know how good it felt to be happy?"

Charles to Mary after John breaks her heart.

("Times of Change")

This scene is a such special father/daughter moment.

"Only God can help you. Just give Him a chance, and He can."

Laura to her friend Ellen's mother after Ellen drowns, and her mother is unsure how to carry on.

("My Ellen")

"I don't think it's silly to worry about other people's feelings."

Caroline to "handyman" Chris, when he expresses concern that maybe she's upset, then calls himself silly for asking.

("The Handyman")

I saw an interview with Karen Grassle during which she said that this episode was really fun for her, because Caroline always has to be a good example for her girls and do the right thing. Then this handsome man falls in love with her, and she gets to shine a little.

"Bandit, you showed up just in the nick of time!"

Alice Garvey, relieved that Laura's dog has come to bring Laura home for supper. Andy and Laura have challenged her to try doing a long jump. Wanting to show them that she's not old, she heads to the starting line. Bandit arrives just before she is about to try it.

("The Wolves")

After Andy goes into the house, Alice decides to try the long jump. She did it, but then fell on her butt. Hersha Parady ("Alice") sent me a photo herself mid-jump in this scene, and wrote, "She WASN'T too old, and DID take that leap!"

Bandit shows up at the Garveys' again later in this episode, to signal to them that the kids are in trouble at the Ingalls' house. A pack of wild wolves is digging under the walls of the barn, where Mary, Carrie, Laura and Andy all are.

"The subject for today's sermon, which I selected several days ago, is based on the twenty-third psalm. 'The Lord is my shepherd. I shall not want. He maketh me to lie down in green pastures!!' "

Reverend Alden beginning the Sunday service and stifling his laughter when he notices that Charles is sitting in the front row, and his hair is green!

("The Creeper of Walnut Grove")

"All right, you're not a miracle worker! Maybe you're not even the best doctor in the world; but she doesn't need the best doctor! She needs you! She needs somebody she can believe in; someone she believes cares what happens to her and her baby. Doc, this is the most important moment in her life."

Charles trying to convince Dr. Baker that he's been wrong to give up his medical practice, especially because one of his patients is desperate for his care.

("To Run and Hide")

"Oh, uh, Broder? Ya got them outlaws, didn't ya?"

Jonathan Garvey after outsmarting a group of bounty hunters who have come to town to kill the James brothers, whom they've heard are in Walnut Grove.

("The Aftermath")

This is an interesting story in which Jesse James and his brother take Mary hostage when they find out they've been discovered hiding out in Walnut Grove.

"Well I hope that being right is enough for you. Because you're sure paying a high price for it. So is Andrew."

The ever-wise Caroline to Alice Garvey when neither she nor Jonathan want to admit fault in their failed marriage.

("The High Cost of Being Right")

Hersha Parady told me that this was a very special episode for her

because it was the first that was written for her character. She did not, however, like the ending (with Judge Picker and all of the laughter)!

I like this line and this scene, because it goes back to the idea of admitting our mistakes. It takes two people to argue, and both can't be "right." Sometimes neither one is "right." But each person definitely has a part in it. Such a valuable idea for families to remember.

"I'll be leaving for Chicago in the morning. Good luck, Joe Kagan."

Joe's wife when he refuses to give up boxing for her and their son, even though the career is killing him.

("The Fighter")

This is a struggle between Joe's desire to do what he loves and needing to find another profession so that he can be there for his family. Varied priorities among people who love each other can cause a great deal of pain. Flexibility is key.

"He risked his life to save it. And all you care about is your balloon. Well you just go to your balloon, and leave us alone."

Mary to a conceited showman after her friend saves Carrie from a hot air balloon that has been cut loose.

("Meet Me at the Fair")

This prestigious guy loses Mary to the nicer boy. Nice is good. Kindness wins.

"I think marriage is a wonderful institution. Ya know, it's a very noble calling for a woman; to be a wife, homemaker, helpmate, keeper of the present, mother of the future . . . Nothing should stand in the way of love! Not people, not position, not money, nothing!"

Miss Beadle, who is considering the marriage proposal she's received, says this to Nellie, not realizing that Nellie is thinking of eloping!

("Here Come the Brides")

When Nellie decides to follow through with the crazy plan, Harriet flips out and tries to shoot the poor kid! "Nels," she says, "make her a widow!!"

Laura: *(to a little Native American girl who is staying in their barn with her family)* **"You don't have to be afraid of me."**

Native American Chief: "She is afraid of the people who killed her mother."

Everyone is silent. Laura is heartbroken and feels so awful for these poor people, living in constant fear of "haters."

("Freedom Flight")

Miss Beadle: "Uh, Laura? Would you like to go to the outhouse?"

Laura: "Yes, Ma'am, I sure would."

Laura wants to impress a new love interest but hasn't developed much yet, so she puts apples in the chest area of her dress. When Laura is called to solve a math problem on the blackboard, one her her apples falls onto the floor.

I also love the talk Caroline has with inconsolable Laura after this traumatic event:

Laura: "I made a fool out of myself yesterday!"

Caroline: "I quite agree!"

Laura: "You do?

Caroline: "Yes. Anyone who pretends to be anybody else is just plain, downright silly."

Laura: "Well, I just want other people – Jimmy Hill – to like me."

Caroline: "Before they can, you have to like yourself. That's the most important thing of all. We have to be – to become – what God intended. If He went to all the trouble to make a Laura Ingalls, He certainly wouldn't want her to act like anybody else. God must like Laura Ingalls an awful lot,

so why shouldn't you? ...I want you to get up and get dressed for school. And I expect you to conduct yourself like Laura Ingalls. Not some poor imitation of somebody else."

("The Rivals")

An amazing voice and lesson that all kids should hear! Caroline truly was the greatest, wisest, most loving mother.

"Do unto others as you would have them do unto you."

Rachel Peel preaching this as the seventh commandment.

("Whisper Country")

She is a mean, awkward and unstable woman who betrays Mary terribly. This saying – The Golden Rule – is the only intelligent thing she really has to offer. Too bad she doesn't live by The Golden Rule. It's a happy ending after Mary sets her straight!

Charles' pa, to him as a boy: "Mr. Watson here says that you roped the school outhouse

shut with him inside. Is that true?"

Charles: "Yes, Sir."

Charles' pa: "Well, then you know what to expect ... Bend over."

He takes off his belt and hands it to Mr. Watson, who smacks Charles several times. After he leaves:

Charles' pa: "I would appreciate with a little less mischief from you, Mr. Charles, and a

little more application to your studies. Why don't you go on into the house, and we'll be going to the berry festival without ya."

("I Remember, I Remember!")

I absolutely love the way Charles' father handled this. There was questioning followed by a calm consequence.

"She'll always be called 'Grace.'"

"Anna" to Laura, who has found the baby Anna left in the woods and has taken care of her while Charles spends weeks trying to locate Anna. Laura has named the baby "Grace" and is thrilled when Anna decides to keep that name for her child. Now Laura knows she will always be remembered by Anna and the baby.

("Be My Friend")

Caroline: "Look, Charles! The Ingalls Carriage Company! We used to make jokes about owning it."

Charles: "That's right, we did!"

Mr. Whitehead: "You do, Mr. Ingalls."

Charles: "I do?! I do . . . ."

A fun interaction right after Charles is told that he's been named heir to his wealthy uncle's estate.

("The Inheritance")

Charles' facial expressions are awesome!

"You're a bunch of nincompoops!"

Peter Lungstrom, the Olesons' well-to-do nephew, when he's teased by the other boys.

("The Stranger")

Sometimes I want to call certain people "nincompoops," too! It's a funny name . . . and very fitting for some folks! Nowadays, our names for nincompoops are not so polite and prairie-esque.

"Caroline Ingalls, we have a problem here . . . . Because we have to name her, and the only names you chose were Graham and Nathaniel. And I *love* you!"

Charles to Caroline, after she gives birth to Grace and has only been willing to believe for the last nine months that the baby will be a boy.

I also love this little scene, which takes place while Laura is helping Andy is fix a barn roof:

Andy: "I suppose your pa wants a boy."

Laura: "What's so great about boys, anyway?"

Andy: "Well, can you fix a barn roof?"

Laura: "Sure! Can *you* have a baby?"

Andy is stumped, and Laura's grin is excellent!

("A Most Precious Gift")

"I remember a talk that I had one night in this church with one of you. He had no answers either. The sight was being taken away from his child for some unexplained reason, and I told him that his daughter was chosen for some very special purpose. I had no idea what it was. Mary Ingalls is going to be leaving us very soon. She's going to teach in a school for the blind. To help other blind children! So now we know what purpose God had in mind."

Reverend Alden's tearful words to the church congregation before the Ingalls move to Winoka.

("I'll Be Waving as You Drive Away")

*These words are so meaningful to me, because I believe that God really does have a grand plan, and that He has chosen a unique purpose for each of us. Sometimes, it is **so** incredibly difficult to imagine what His plan could **possibly** be; especially when we face tragedy, loss, and hardship. If we have faith, God will show us.*

"I have to be honest. I know what's in the package. Ma and I talked it over, and I hope you understand. I know what you were trying to do, but the greatest present you could give me is to be able to hear you play this fiddle on my birthday. It always has been. I love you, Pa."

Mary on her sixteenth birthday, after she finds out that Charles sold his fiddle so he could buy her a fancy new hat.

Pa's fiddle plays a subtle yet amazingly meaningful role in Little House. In this scene, it's so terrific, and I feel it's symbolic of the episode's title, "As Long as We're Together." Alice Garvey has already toasted to friendship in an earlier scene, saying, **"It was awfully scary coming here to the city, not knowing what to expect.**

But no matter what, I know it'll work out, and I'm not afraid anymore. Because we got somethin' here that's just about the most important thing in the world. True friends." *This is a wonderful, lifelong message for all of us to keep in mind. When Charles plays his fiddle at Mary's birthday celebration, it surely brings the family (and the audience) back to peaceful evenings in the little house on Plum Creek. To me this represents the Ingalls' belief that they really are "home" as long as they have each other and their friends.*

("As Long as We're Together")

"The record books show that the first forward pass in football was thrown on October 3, 1906 in New Haven. But *I* happen to know that the first forward pass of a *human being* was thrown on November 29, 1880 in Winoka. I know because I was *there*; and *saw it!*"

Laura reflecting on the unbelievable play that helped the Winoka Warriors defeat the Dakota Dragons.

("The Winoka Warriors")

"The point isn't whether you knew or not, is it? The point is that we should never make unkind remarks about anyone. I'm sure when you see Amelia tomorrow, you'll apologize. You thought of the jokes. You can think of an apology."

Caroline's response when Laura tells her that she and her friends made fun of an overweight man and then found out that the man was their new friend's father.

("The Man Inside")

Caroline handles this so well. She is understanding but doesn't show a ton of sympathy, because what the kids did was mean. She is amazing:

Laura: "It wasn't only me."

Caroline: "Oh, you know better than to use an excuse like that."

Laura: "I really am sorry, Ma."

Caroline: "The way to show that is to try to never do it again."

I have stolen that last line from Caroline and used it with my own children. Kids tend to say they're sorry automatically, because they've been programmed to. It's important, though, for them to identify what they're really sorry about and to be reminded not to repeat their mistakes.

Charles: "We'll start cleaning up in a minute. First, I want everybody to just listen. Just *listen*."

Laura: "I don't hear anything ... except maybe a bird."

Charles: "Well that's just the point. It's quiet. For the first time in months, it's really quiet."

Caroline: "Amen."

The Ingalls family, as soon as they walk in the door of their house after their long trip home from Winoka.

("There's No Place like Home")

I love how relieved and overjoyed they are to be back in Walnut Grove, in their little house. Home really should be a place where we feel happy.

"I love you more than anything, and I just took it for granted that you knew that. It was dumb of me for not telling you how much I love you. 'Cause I love you more than anything. I do."

Charles admitting that he's inadvertently neglected Laura in order to spend time with Albert and make him feel comfortable living with them.

("Fagin")

A great apology after a great lesson learned by a parent!

Harriet: "I wanna know, *how* are they being punished?"

Caroline: "They can't work for the paper anymore."

Harriet: "Of course they can't work for the paper anymore! Good grief, Woman! They should be horsewhipped for what they did! Telling those monstrous lies about me and Nellie!"

Caroline: "Well, if the items were wrong – and I don't know that they weren't –"

Harriet: "If?! Of course they were wrong!"

Caroline: "Then you can always print a retraction. Put it right on the front page; don't stick it way in the back. Something to the effect of, ummm . . . contrary to published reports, Harriet Oleson does *not* have false teeth and does *not* wear a wig."

Caroline, giving Harriet a taste of her own medicine, after "false news" has been printed repeatedly in the town newspaper.

("Harriet's Happenings")

BWA ha ha ha ha! This scene is SO well done by both actresses! Their disdain for each other is bubbling over!

"That's the difference between us. If there's something I have to do, I do it. I don't just give up!"

Adam to Mary, after she's called off their wedding for fear of not being able to properly care for a sighted child if they have one. Now, as they're searching for one of their blind students during a sand storm, Mary expresses doubt about finding her.

("The Wedding")

I always liked how Little House didn't allow Mary and Adam's blindness to stop them from living a productive life and doing great things. This is a powerful message to our children (and to all of us!), as is Adam's message to Mary about persevering.

Andy: "Ya know, Pa, I don't care that much about bein' a man just yet."

Albert: "Me neither. I kinda just like bein' your boy."

After the boys have passed their "test" proving they're old enough to do "a man's work."

("Men Will Be Boys")

Harriet: "How dare you disgrace me like this?!"

Nellie: "But you said I was just like you!"

Harriet to Nellie, after Alice Garvey reveals to her that Nellie has been cheating on all of her tests.

("The Cheaters")

I feel like this episode ranks toward the top of those in which we most love to hate Nellie. She was ROUGH! Alison Arngrim really did OWN that part; she was absolutely ***phenomenal****! I also love the part of this episode where she tells Andy that she cheats:* **"Who can remember all those things they want you to?? Just clutters the mind."** *This line and Alison's facial expression make giggle every time I see it. She was brilliant! This is a great episode, for so many reasons.*

"Come along, Samson."

Harriet, finally accepting this little black boy as a person; one of her friends.

("Blind Journey")

This ending really tugs at the heartstrings. A phenomenal lesson in considering other perspectives and cultures, and a great example of how children can open our minds.

Nellie: "*Does* Mr. Singerman have horns on his head?"

Albert: "I don't know. He never takes off his hat."

Nellie (and Albert, for that matter) questioning the rumors around school that say Jewish people have horns on their heads.

("The Craftsman")

What's humorous about this is that it's so ridiculous; and Albert knows that, so he decides to play a joke on Nellie and Willie. He gets Laura involved, too. Albert tells Nellie and Willie that Mr. Singerman does have horns on his head, and that they can come see for themselves. When they approach Mr. Singerman's barn, the door opens, and a huge set of antlers pokes out! Those snotty Oleson kids nearly soil their pants. Nice!

"There's lots I don't remember."

Jordan Harrison, after a huge ordeal in which he falls out of a tree and can't see at first; then he regains his vision but fakes being blind in order to keep his ever-fighting parents together. Next, he falls off a horse and hits his head, causing him to forget that he'd been pretending.

("Blind Man's Bluff")

Whew! There's a lot going on here! Hopefully none of our kids will try this!

"Kiss me! Kiiisssss Me!"

My goodness, this episode is comical. Toby Noe (played by Ray Bolger, who also played the Scarecrow in *The Wizard of Oz, 1939*) is interested in a stuffy, bitter old woman and tries to make her jealous by having a picnic lunch outside her house with a very desperate female. She basically attacks him with affection!

("Dance With Me")

Wendi Lou Lee, who played Grace Ingalls, told me, "My favorite episode of all time is 'Dance With Me' from season five. It features the legendary Ray Bolger as Toby Noe, trying to swoon the widow, Miss Cooper. I share a scene with Ray out in front of the Ingalls house. He's spilling his heart to a baby sitting in her highchair. I love it so much that I named my son Tobey in honor of Ray and our time together."

This scene is hysterical! I love Wendi's sweet memory; and how special it is that she named her son Tobey!

"You still can't stand to look at me, can you? Goodbye, Father."

Adam after his father has come to Walnut Grove when he hears Mary is going to have a baby, convinces Adam and Mary to move to New York with him, and then reneges when Mary miscarries.

("The Sound of Children")

Adam's father is such a jerk of a guy.

"*You've* got the *GUN!!*"

Nellie screaming back at her mother, who is yelling at her to "Kill it! Shoot it!" Laura, Albert, Andy, and Kezia have convinced Harriet, Nellie, and Willie that there is a monster in the lake where they've rented a summer home.

("The Lake Kezia Monster")

"Mr. Larabee. He could've set the fire. I'm not sayin' that he couldn't have come back and done it. But it could've been me, too."

Andy Garvey, right before the jury decides the fate of a hateful man who has betrayed his neighbors and then beat up on Andy. Though he knows that Larabee is guilty of hurting him, he's not sure that the man burned down the Garveys' barn, a crime of which he is being accused.

("Barn Burner")

Such a brave move and an example to all kids about doing the right thing.

A very meaningful part of the storyline in this terrific episode revolves around the character of Joe Kagan, a black gentleman who has been accepted into the church of Walnut Grove, yet not accepted by all members of the congregation. When Joe is appointed to the jury in the Garvey vs. Larabee case, he is the only member who does not vote that Mr. Larabee is guilty of barn-burning. He says that he cannot change his mind unless someone says they actually saw Larabee actually do it. When the judge asks him to step down and be replaced, he insists on "saying his piece":

"I gotta live my life the best way I can, knowing that the Larabees of this world are looking at me and my kind with hatred in their hearts. I can't change that. But I gotta believe in the law. And I gotta believe in justice. And I gotta believe that it applies to each and every one of us, including Mr. Larabee. I guess maybe I'm different. For less reason than you've convicted a man of burning a barn that nobody saw him burn, I've seen my people with ropes around their necks, hangin' dead. And that's what makes me different. 'Cause I can't erase those pictures from my brain. I know what can happen when justice disappears. And I will bring harm to no man when his guilt ain't been proven in my eyes."

So very powerful. So unbelievably important.

"Pink and ... purple? Gee, Laura, I'm kinda glad I *can't* see it ..."

Mary reacting to the colors that Laura and Albert have painted their "clubhouse," after she returns from a series of eye exams with the hope of regaining her sight.

("The Enchanted Cottage")

"You need someone. You've needed someone for a long time. Leslie, needing and loving just aren't the same thing. The things you see in me are the things you *used* to see in your husband. Remember I told you once that a person has to work at being happy? I think your husband's ready for that work."

Charles, speaking to Leslie, a neglected wife who has become enamored with him after years of being neglected by her husband.

("Someone Please Love Me")

Charles is portrayed as the most magical husband and father ever! I kinda feel sorry for the 1970s and 80s hubby-dads out there who had to try to measure up! Sheesh!

Charles: "Caroline's at the blind school. They've turned it into a hospital."

Jonathan: "What is it?"

Charles: "Anthrax."

The two men wind up traveling to get medicine for all of the people who have become ill in Walnut Grove.

("Mortal Mission")

This isn't one of my favorite episodes, probably because it paints a brutal picture of what pioneers really had to face in those days. It isn't as happy-go-lucky as some of the other shows; but that's the point. This was their existence. A hard, rugged, often-frightening life. All of these factors make this episode a very important one to watch.

"It's just like I pictured it. It runs right into the sky. It doesn't have an end ... I'd like to walk from here .... Thank you all."

Dillon, a terminally ill boy whom Charles, Laura, and Albert help to achieve his dream of seeing the ocean.

("The Odyssey")

This episode always makes me wonder what I would want to do if I found out I only had a month to live. Powerful. Frightening. Empowering. Thought-Provoking.

Laura: "He's so sure that the new teacher's gonna be pretty, he's in love with her already!

Albert: "That's dumb!"

Laura: "No dumber than wearin' a tie to school!"

Charles: "All right, let's stop talkin' about who's the dumbest. Why don't we get ourselves to school and find out who can be the smartest."

Charles handling first-day-of-school nerves and bickering.

("Back to School")

It's ironic that Laura is ribbing Albert so much about wanting to impress a female, because in this episode, she meets and becomes immediately crazy about Almanzo.

"I guess you're stuck with me … Pa."

Albert to Charles after his real father has tried to regain custody of him.

The always quick-thinking Albert pretends to be blind when he meets the man, because he isn't convinced his father really wants him for the right reasons.

("The Family Tree")

Slick move, Dude! This scene, both acting and writing, was absolutely brilliant.

"I can feel the sun on my face. It's west of us."

Mary to Adam after their stage coach crashes, leaving Adam pinned underneath and a pregnant woman inside it. Mary needs to go find help, despite her blindness.

("The Third Miracle")

*This line always struck me, because I have the worst sense of direction known (or should I say "unknown") to man. Leave it to a pioneer girl to feel the heat of the sun and know where she's located. I **have** my eyesight and couldn't find my way out of a paper bag, even if I had a map. Impressive, Mary! I hope my kids have a* *better sense of direction than I do. Guess I better teach them how to "read" the sun (once **I** figure it out).*

"Que sera, sera."

Circus master, London, to Laura when she tells him that she loves Almanzo and just wants him to wait for her to be old enough so they can be together.

("Annabelle")

This is a fun part, because up until this moment, London was just "the sad clown" who never talked. He reveals himself to Laura now, with the words that mean "whatever will be, will be." We can't predict the future or force things to happen. We just have to have faith that everything works out the way it's supposed to. For Laura, as we all know, things ***do*** *work out for the best!*

"I'm a man, Charles, with all the flesh and blood and spiritual needs of man; and all the doubts and the uncertainty. No, the only time I feel needed is an hour or two on Sunday, at marriages and deaths. Charles, I need to be needed on a regular basis. Not just fall into the cracks between other people's joys and sorrows. Moving about from town to town, I am so tired of spending lonely nights in cold empty rooms listening only to my breathing."

Reverend Alden telling Charles that he's thinking about getting married.

("The Preacher Takes a Wife.")

Happily, a minister ***can*** *get married, and I think Reverend Alden deserves that companionship! In fact, I think anyone who wants to share his or her life with someone should be able to experience that joy. No one deserves to be lonely.*

"Relax?! I've been standing here for an hour while she's been using me as a pin cushion, and she tells me to relax."

Albert, while Laura is pinning his Halloween headpiece on him.

("The Halloween Dream")

Isaiah: "God Almighty, Man, I thought you were dying! I almost killed myself gettin' back here to save ya!"

Charles: "Well, I thought killing yourself was your idea in the first place! I had a hard time keeping up with you. You move pretty good when you're thinking about someone besides yourself."

Charles, knocking sense into his best friend, who has been crippled in an accident and is now suicidal.

("The Return of Mr. Edwards")

Charles has a good point. Sometimes we tend to work harder for others' well-being than we do for our own. ***WE*** *are worth our best efforts, too.*

"Oh, Nels. I am the church treasurer, and it's not gambling. Gambling is when you can lose. Now, Big John can't lose! He already beat the man once, and he's gonna beat him again! And I'm gonna double the church fund! Please just get out of here and let me do the Lord's work!"

Harriet arguing with Nels, who is trying to talk her out of using the congregation's money to bet on Jonathan Garvey in a wrestling match against a professional.

("The King is Dead")

As you can probably guess, she doesn't listen to Nels. Piece of work!

"Gimme your crutches, Brother! You don't need 'em!"

Charles to an actor who has been hired by a scam artist to pretend he has been cured of his paralysis.

("The Faith Healer")

This scam artist comes to Walnut Grove and essentially "steals" Reverend Alden's congregation by manipulating people to think he can cure the sick. Along comes good ole Charles. Always the hero!

"I came back to thank you. My pa's been real busy lately, and he hasn't actually read the book himself. I'm hopin' he never finds out what's in it; stuff about my ma. I can't believe that my own grandfather would write

such things down for the whole world to see! There's this one part where my ma was in a public place, and she . . . wasn't wearing anything . . . Naked. So ya see why I didn't want folks to be readin' that book?"

Sly little Albert! Acting as though Harriet did the Ingalls a favor when she refused to carry his grandfather's new book in the mercantile, he outsmarts her.

("Author! Author!)

What she doesn't know (until she suddenly does a 180 and offers to buy every copy of the book) is that, in the part of the story he's referring to, Caroline is only a baby.

"Somebody sneezed!"

Mr. Anderson, after a phone conversation to which Harriet is listening through the switchboard. Albert tells him, "Mrs. Oleson also has hay fever."

("Crossed Connections")

The two of them decide to teach her a lesson, which is ***always*** *fun!*

This earlier conversation between Harriet and Nellie always makes me giggle as well:

Harriet: "I swear; I will never understand that woman (Caroline) as long as I live! It's one thing to be poor, but it's another thing to admit it."

Nellie: "Well, poor people are ignorant, Mother. That's why they never amount to anything."

Harriet: "How true, how true! Thank heavens we're rich!"

Nellie: "Amen."

"Everybody needs somebody."

Charles to an ornery teenager who is staying with the Ingalls while he works off a watch he stole from Charles.

("The Angry Heart")

Ornery teens are really charming, aren't they? My son, who used to look at me adoringly now gives me the side eye and calls me "Bruh." Good times.

"There isn't anything that any *one* person can do; but there's plenty that *all* of us can do."

Laura trying to convince her schoolmates that they have to stick together to put the class bully in his place and stop their teacher from leaving town.

("The Werewolf of Walnut Grove")

Teamwork is such an important skill for children to learn. Not only does it help get big things accomplished, but it's healthy for the individual to learn how to mesh with others and be open to new ideas and ways of doing things.

"If that isn't success, I don't know what is."

Charles to Caroline when they arrive home from a disheartening school reunion, and their children all coming running out of the house to hug them.

("What Ever Happened to the Class of '56?")

They experience feelings similar to many people who attend school reunions, where everyone tends to want to prove how rich, important, thin, or successful they are. What Charles and Caroline realize most is how their love has grown over the years, and what a beautiful family they're raising. They find this much more valuable than all the money their classmates have. The chemistry between Caroline and Charles here is really great. Michael Landon and Karen Grassle were always outstanding at projecting the true love that existed between their characters.

Mary: "Do you remember the time we went camping with the Olesons?"

Laura: "How could I forget?!"

The girls (now women) reminiscing about their childhood when Laura stays overnight with Mary at the blind school.

("Darkness Is My Friend")

I don't usually watch this episode, because it's scary! This fun little conversation between Laura and Mary is one of the only cheerful parts. After it, three criminals force their way in, and it gets ugly from there. I remember when this episode aired, my great grandma was babysitting for me. As we were watching it, someone knocked at the front door. Great Grandma asked me to come with her to answer it. We were both freaked out!

"Sharing your life with someone is fine, but you gotta to love them. You can't pretend to feel something you don't feel."

Charles explaining to Laura that it's not right to accept another boy's affections just because Almanzo isn't interested in her.

("Silent Promises")

Becoming involved with someone solely because we want to help him or her, rather than because we love him or her, isn't fair to anyone. There has to be mutual love and respect.

"If she *was* here right now, what do you think she would she say to you? She'd say, 'Jonathan Garvey, what in God's name is wrong with you?' That's what she'd say. She'd say, 'What's wrong with the man I love?' "

Charles trying to help Jonathan manage his anger and care for his son after Alice dies in a fire.

("May We Make Them Proud")

When we lose loved ones, life goes on, but it takes time for us to learn to live without them. Thank goodness for the support of family members and friends to help us through these times. We have to remember to lean on them.

"Laura, I can't tell you how tired I am of hearing about Almanzo."

Charles, when Laura's adoration of "Manly" begins to get on Charles' nerves.

("Wilder and Wilder")

***He** wants to keep being the man in Half-Pint's life!*

"God, deliver thee from thy family! And other fools!"

Nels blowing his top when Harriet, Nellie, and Willie finally drive him crazy enough to leave town and start a new business venture on his own.

("Second Spring")

Nels.Oleson.Is.A.Saint. !!!

"You look different. You look *older*."

Almanzo to Laura, the first time he looks at her and sees a grown woman.

("Sweet Sixteen")

Woot! It's about time, "Zaldamo!"

"You *LOVE* him?!?!?! You can't love him, he's too SHORT!"

Harriet, when Nellie is in tears because she's in love with Percival, and he's leaving town.

This conversation gets even funnier:

Nellie: "He's not too short. I'm too tall."

Harriet: "Well don't blame me. It's your father's fault. Everybody's tall on his side of the family.

Nels: "Your mother's right. Her side is just fat."

("He Loves Me, He Loves Me Not")

Classic. Richard Bull had amazing delivery and facial expressions!

"I know how you're feeling. But don't worry; you'll be a teacher ... A mother is all things. A cook, a dressmaker, a disciplinarian, a nurse ... But above all a teacher. And when your children are ready to graduate from your family, they'll be as ready to face the world as you are. I know they will."

Caroline to Laura, who has realized that once she marries Almanzo, she won't be able to teach.

("Laura Ingalls Wilder")

I've always loved this little mother/daughter chat. Caroline makes all the right points and gives a great list of motherly roles. Nowadays, she could add taxi service, referee, and text-affiliated social coordinator. We wear a lot of hats (or should I say "bonnets?"). How many am I missing?

"When you lose somebody like your ma, it leaves some awful scars, because we loved her so much, and she was so special. We're gonna hurt for a while, but in time, we won't blame anybody."

Jonathan to Andy, who is missing Alice. In this scene, Andy is feeling angry with Mary and Adam, because Alice died trying to save their baby. Jonathan reminds him that, right after Alice passed away, he was blaming God.

("A New Beginning")

Little House gives so many positive, faith-filled thoughts on grieving. These are so significant, as death is a part of life, and we all need to find ways to cope. When children lose a parent – or any loved one – they search for signs that they're going to be okay. It's important for us to provide those signs.

"What kinda man are you?"

Charles, obviously holding himself back from decking Albert's football coach when Albert gets hurt, and his coach doesn't take him out of the game.

("Fight Team, Fight!")

Winning ***isn't*** *everything.*

"Well, it's not true that Josh don't make a sound. Oh, it ain't talk, but I heard it. It's fillin' this whole room right now. You don't hear it with your ears. You hear it with your heart. It's a silent cry; a cry of love."

Houston Lam pleading with the head of the orphanage and a boy's prospective parents to accept Josh, even though he is a selective mute.

("The Silent Cry")

Sniffle, sniffle. Another tear-jerker for sure.

"This is different. This Mr. Unger liked my paintings *before* he knew I was blind. No one wants to hurt a blind person. Now I know for sure, they must look like they do in my mind."

Annie Crane, giving Caroline an interesting perspective about wondering whether people compliment her artwork because she's blind or because it's actually good.

("Portrait of Love")

"I'm on the side of making sure this is not a misunderstanding before I do Almanzo Wilder great bodily harm."

Charles, to Caroline and Laura, who think Almanzo is having an affair with a girl who lives in town and was always interested in him.

("Divorce Walnut Grove Style")

I've always found this line to be hysterical (and oh, so fatherly). The situation is, of course, a misunderstanding, but before Laura knows this, she gets into a big fight with the girl. Right in the middle of the street by Nellie's restaurant, they roll on the ground, bloomers showing and everything!

"You taught me a good lesson. From now on, I'm gonna be honest about myself. You taught me somethin' else, too; and that's that some folks love different from others … I still love you, and I would no matter what. 'Cause that's what really lovin' is."

Albert meeting his pen pal, Leslie. Neither of them has been honest with the other about his/her true self.

("Dearest Albert, I'll Miss You")

I think it's vital for our children to know that fabricating untruths about ourselves is never a good idea. There's no shame in being who we are. Our real friends will like us that way!

"Do you know what your father's planning to do? *(chuckling)* **He's planning to take a shortcut across the prairie.** *(giggling)* **He doesn't know where he might wind up.** *(laughing hysterically)* **He could end up in the middle of a bog, smack in the middle of nowhere!"**

Caroline to Laura, who, in turn, shares that Almanzo has such a big load on his wagon, it'll be hard to get it up a hill. Laura is also laughing. The men have a bet to see who can get to Sleepy Eye faster.

("The In-Laws")

I enjoy this scene so much, because Caroline and Laura wind up laughing so hard, and I get to laugh with them! It's fun each time.

"Jonathan. Jonathan! I can see. I can SEE!"

Adam, just after he opens his eyes following an accident and realizes he's regained his eyesight. He recognizes Jonathan by voice.

("To See the Light")

This scene makes me so happy, every time I watch it! I can't imagine the joy that would come from regaining my eyesight after being blind for so long! And Adam's reaction when he first sees Mary is wonderful, too!

The side story in this episode is a lot of fun; Harriet tries (unsuccessfully) to lose weight when she finds out her ever-slim cousin is coming to visit:

Percival: "I'm sorry, Mrs. Oleson, but the truth is the truth."

Harriet: "Oh, is that so? Well, for your information, Young Man, I'm not fat. I'm large-boned."

Percival: "That would be very difficult to determine, since your bones are buried so deep beneath the surface!"

Harriet: (gasping) **"Nellie! Are you going to stand there and let this little thing insult your mother like that?"**

Nellie: "I have to, Mother. He's right."

BWA HA HA HA HA! Wow, Percival. Well, Harriet doesn't want to take Nellie's word for it. So she goes to Nels (… Bad idea):

Harriet: "Nels?"

Nels: "Yes, Dear."

Harriet: "Can I ask you a question?"

Nels: "Yes, Dear."

Harriet: "Do you think I'm fat?"

Nels: "Yes, Dear."

Harriet: (again, gasping) **"Nels! I'm talking to you! How dare you say that I'm fat!"**

Nels: "How dare you *ask* if you're fat?"

Harriet starts in with her hilarious blubbering, which becomes even funnier when Nels tells her that she's "pleasingly plump." GREAT scene!

"I'm going away for a few days . . . to Nellie's . . . to have a little adventure and to prove something to your father. Now, while I'm gone, I want you to just be yourselves and have a good time. Oh, listen. If you need to talk to me, just come by Nellie's. I'll be there, any time of the day. Oh, and remember, have a good time!"

Caroline to Albert, Carrie, and Grace as she leaves to join all the women in town and try to get their husbands to realize how much women do. They want the men to sign a petition for equal shares of all property.

("Oleson vs. Oleson")

This one is interesting because it touches on equality for women, which has come a long way in the last 150 years, but is still an issue today. As women all over the United States argue for the same salaries earned by men, it still isn't the case in many professions. At the end, Charles does sign the petition, and the other men in town follow. He tells Caroline, **"I just decided we're on the same team."** *The episode ends with Laura's voice saying,* **"Ma had won her fight. The petition was on its way to the legislature. She says someday women will even have the right to vote! Maybe, but I doubt it."**

How far we've come!

"Is this what religion is all about? Anger? Fighting? Hatred? Well, if it is, Nellie and I don't want any part of it."

Nellie's husband, Percival, telling his parents and in-laws to stop being stubborn fools about the religion of their baby.

("Come, Let Us Reason Together")

This episode exemplifies some of the difficulties that can emerge when religions mix through marriage. Nels has a creative solution, which Nellie and Percival find hilariously ridiculous!

"It's impossible to scare someone to death ..."

Myron Wilder, Almanzo's conniving nephew responding to Almanzo's scolding.

("The Nephews")

These two boys. Grrrrrrr! Myron and Rupert come to stay with Laura and Almanzo while their parents take a second honeymoon, and boy, do the adult Wilders have their work cut out for them! Burping in church, starting fires in the yard, and plucking the feathers out of all their chickens? Ugh!

"Well, I guess I'll have to see how you work out!"

Hester Sue, when she calls off her wedding in the middle of the ceremony and acknowledges that she loves Joe Kagan.

("Make a Joyful Noise")

The little boy who played rebellious Timothy in this episode was Keith Coogan, and I had a little crush on him when he starred in Adventures in Babysitting (1987) with Elisabeth Shue.

"Ralph, would you please stand in the corner? You were pulling Willie's hair. We don't

do that here . . . . Have you ever heard of peripheral vision? Well, I have it. It means that I can see out of the corner of my eye, and I saw you pull Willie's hair. Now do you want to sit there and argue with me, or do you want to stand in the corner and get it over with?!"

Laura to newcomer and troublemaker, Ralph, in the schoolhouse.

(Goodbye, Mrs. Wilder")

The best part of this is Willie's reaction. Willie is ***always*** *in the corner at school, so he's amazed when Laura believes him and puts someone* ***else*** *in the corner for a change.*

"Mrs. Oleson, on Sunday I will go to church, and I will ask God to forgive me for this (she shoves a ball of bread dough into Harriet's face, and then looks much more relaxed). "But, to tell you the truth, I think the good Lord would have done the same thing!"

Caroline to Harriet, after Harriet spreads a rumor that Albert got a girl pregnant, and then shows up at the restaurant with baby clothes to give to Caroline for her "grandchild."

("Sylvia")

I have always found this to be Little House's most disturbing episode.

Mr. Davis: "Adam! That was a heck of a job!"

Adam: "Why, thank you!"

Mr. Davis: "Listen, why don't you and I have a meeting tomorrow. I think there's a very good chance I can find a spot for you in my law firm."

Adam: "No, I'm very sorry, but I think my partner and I would rather go it alone."

Mr. Davis: "Look Son, I can make you a much better offer than anything your partner can do."

Adam: "No, I don't think you can. *(to Mary)* **Let's go to lunch, Partner!"**

"Mr. Davis" is the owner of a Sleepy Eye law firm, who has promised Adam a job when he finishes law school but refuses him one when the time comes.

Adam chooses to be Walnut Grove's lawyer, with Mary as his assistant. Now, when Adam wins his first big court case, the guy suddenly has a spot open for him.

("Blind Justice")

It's so satisfying when Adam turns ***him*** *down this time. Later, Sir!*

"Oh, I don't know if this is the right time to tell you! I was going to tell you tonight at supper anyway. Ya know, I think Laura's baby is gonna have an uncle the same age. I'm pregnant too!"

Caroline, telling Charles, Laura, and Almanzo that she's pregnant. Unfortunately, she isn't. Instead, she's going through "the change," as they called it on the prairie.

("I Do, Again")

Caroline has a horrible time accepting this news. She's devastated about the fact that she'll never be able to give Charles a son. Charles later wins us over (for the 697th time), when he reminds Caroline of his undying love and assures her that she means more to him than anything in the world.

When I look at this episode today, with the eyes of a middle-aged woman who is also "going through the change," I admire Caroline's desire to continue to have children. My desires at this point in my life include cooling off the hot flashes, covering up my dark eye circles, avoiding inevitable belly fat, and reversing sagginess. Oh, and I'd rather not pee every time I cough or sneeze. Too much to ask? Landsakes . . . Compared to Caroline, I sound like an ungrateful, OLD grouch.

"When I say 'home,' I mean our place. We want you to come live with us. Isn't that right Caroline? It's gonna be pretty darn crowded, but that's just the way it's gonna be."

Charles telling James and Cassandra that they don't have to go back to their evil adoptive family but are welcome – and wanted – at the Ingalls' house forever.

("The Lost Ones")

I loved the addition of James and Cassandra to the show. Good storylines!

"Nancy sat in that booth the whole day. And a lot of kids said she was a good sport to do it. Well, we knew she'd still be nasty, but she'd be better. Because she knew that folks cared enough about her not to let her get away with things she shouldn't. So just remember that the next time your folks punish you."

Laura's voice at the end of the episode where the Olesons replace Nellie by adopting Nancy, only to have her wreak havoc in their home and at school.

("The Reincarnation of Nellie")

Laura, who is the school teacher, decides to teach Nancy a lesson by sparking her interest in being "the mermaid" at the school bizarre ... which is really "code" for sitting in a dunk tank. Even Mrs. Oleson gets in line to see her sink! This narration is great, too. I remember having a huge smile on my face the night it aired, because it felt so personal, as if Laura was actually talking to me.

"Albert? It's a good thing Laura and Carrie didn't feel that way when you first came to live with us."

Charles to Albert when he's resentful that James is hanging around him all the time and getting away with more than he thinks James should.

("Growin' Pains")

How quickly Albert has forgotten what it was like to feel uncertain of his place in the family. Glad Charles sets him straight here.

"Two weeks ago, a new doctor arrived in Walnut Grove; you're all aware of that. Dr. LeDoux and his wife, Maddie, were introduced to you by Reverend Alden in this church. I was to make that introduction; but I didn't. I told Reverend Alden that I had a house call to make. That was not the truth. I also told Dr. LeDoux that I felt it was wrong to recommend him to you until I'd had a chance to see his work. That too was a lie. I had no reason to doubt the ability of a man who'd studied seventeen years of his life to become a doctor and a surgeon. No reason except one. Prejudice. It was very difficult for me to admit that to myself. Ya see, I'd always thought of myself as a good Christian, a decent, fair human being. But the truth of the matter was, I didn't believe that a black man could become a good doctor. A good man, yes. A good farmer, blacksmith . . . But a doctor? No. That territory belonged to the white man. So I avoided introducing him to you, and I didn't recommend that you see him. Two nights ago, Dr. Le Doux saved the lives of Jenny Sherman and her newborn child. It took a doctor, a surgeon of his skill, to do that. I don't have that skill. Yesterday, Dr. LeDoux told me that he was leaving Walnut Grove to practice in a place that appreciated him. A reasonable decision – understandable – that I feel responsible for. So I want to publicly apologize to Dr. LeDoux, to his wife, Maddie, and to all of you, for bringing it about."

Dr. Baker addressing the congregation and admitting his prejudice and envy of his new associate.

("Dark Sage")

It takes a great deal of courage to do something like this, but I think it's true what they say: "The truth shall set you free." The message here about prejudice is so valuable. I think it's remarkable that Little House continued to touch on this very important topic throughout the series' entire run.

Mort: "Excuse me. You've made a mistake. I was just looking over Laura's paper here, and uh, it's perfect ..."

William: "You're certainly entitled to your opinion, but I am the professor, and I might remind you, a graduate of Yale University."

Mort: "Oh, well, that explains it. See, I'm a Harvard man, myself."

William: "And I did my post-graduate work at Cambridge."

Mort: "Oh. I was at Oxford."

William: "Captain of the debating team. Two years!"

Mort: "Literary Magazine. Editor. Three years.

William: "Perhaps you'd like to step outside and settle this like a man."

Mort: "Not really."

William: "I thought not."

Mort: "But I will."

An argument between Laura's classmate ("Mort") and the professor ("William") of the writing seminar they're taking. William has shown romantic interest in Laura, and when she turns him down, her grade suffers. Mort has had enough of William's pompous attitude. When they head outside:

William: "I hope this is going to be a lesson to you ... Because you are an insufferable, odious lout!"

Mort decks him.

Mort: "I may be an insufferable, odious lout ... but I'm one heck of a boxer!"

("A Wiser Heart")

"Gee. I wonder what went wrong."

Willie, after making his own cannon and basically blowing up the mercantile's storeroom by accident.

("Gambini the Great")

Max: "No way to get our hands on the money, and now two more people to feed!"

Nels: "Maybe this ransom angle isn't gonna work for us. There must be some other way we can come up with the money.

Max: "All I know is, we gotta come up with somethin' fast, 'cause it's gettin' awful crowded in the hideout, ya know what I mean?"

Nels: "What if we break into the bank and *steal* the money?"

Max: "Yeah. I like it. It's quick, it's simple, I like it. Got any Dynamite?"

Nels: "No, but Bill Anderson has got the key to the front door!"

Max: "Key? We use the key? We use the key to get in the front door! Aha ha ha ha! I'm tellin' ya, Nels, you've got what it takes! You could be a regular Jesse James! You're so smart!"

Nels: "Ha! Thanks, Max!"

One of many conversations between Nels and a dopey criminal who holds him (and eventually half the town!) for ransom in a cave near Walnut Grove.

This is a silly, light, just plain fun episode! I've always loved it, because it's so goofy it just makes me laugh. It gets more and more ridiculous as it goes on. Little House dealt with so many serious issues that once in a while, it was really entertaining to see an episode like this.

("The Legend of Black Jake")

"Mr. Callahan? I ain't seen no ring."

Young "BJ Jackson," who helps Isaiah and Charles figure out who murdered John.

("Chicago")

This is a dark episode, but its suspense is luring. BJ is a little boy with a lot of spunk and a lot of street smarts. He describes to Isaiah, Charles, and Mr. Callahan the man he saw when he found John lying dead in an alley. When they find and question the man, he denies killing John. Mr. Callahan grabs the man's hand and says to BJ, "That's the ring you described, Son. Lion's head with ruby eyes. That's it, ain't it?" BJ catches on and agrees, even though he'd never noticed the man's ring on the night of the murder. Slick!

"We hope you'll give us what we never gave you; a chance."

Albert asking Elmer to reconsider his decision to quit school after being bullied by Nancy and teased by the other kids.

("For the Love of Nancy")

Elmer is a sweet character. You root for him as you watch this episode. He makes the mistake of not telling the kids to knock it off with the fat jokes, but rather challenging them to eating contests and encouraging them to call him "Blubber." He's so desperate to fit in that he pretends the teasing doesn't bother him. Finally, he cracks, just like anyone would.

"There's only one thing we can do. Get bigger pockets."

Albert to James, as they meet behind the house to empty their pockets of Charles' awful dinner. Because Caroline is working constantly at the restaurant, Charles is making dinner every night and has told the kids that whoever complains will have to do the cooking the next night.

("The Wave of the Future")

This one is a fave of mine! Harriet accepts a business proposition from a man who basically sells her on the idea of changing Nellie's restaurant into a fast food joint. It's one chuckle after another as the situation worsens with time. Cute ending, too, as a man resembling the colonel of Kentucky Fried Chicken arrives trying to promote his idea of a restaurant that only serves one meal: fried chicken.

Caroline: "I can see why that's a Christmas you'll never forget."
Hester Sue: "And so is this one, because I'm with people I love."

When the Ingalls get snowed in on Christmas Eve, they sit around telling stories from Christmas' past.

("A Christmas They Never Forgot")

This is fun, because everyone recounts tales from their childhoods, which lets us see them as kids and gives us more insight into the characters' pasts.

"I brought you this apple. Aren't you hungry? Look. I'll let you go and I'll give you this apple, but you have to listen to me for the time it takes you to eat it. All right? Just that long."

Caroline to Gideon, who has quit school and run away from home because the kids make fun of his stutter.

("No Beast So Fierce")

Amazing Caroline again, this time coming up with the simple but brilliant idea of bringing a snack to a hungry boy so she can have time to reason with him. ***Love*** *her!*

"Well, if you're waiting for me to tell you what the story means, you're just going to have to figure that out for yourselves."

Caroline to the kids at school after telling them a story that prompts them to work together to help others.

("Stone Soup")

Sometimes it's good to "plant a seed" in our children's heads and let it grow in their minds, rather than figuring everything out for them.

"Ya know why I started all this? All this working? Because I wanted to be remembered. My initials on a piece of furniture. I wanted strangers to remember me. I wasn't even giving my own children a chance to remember me."

Charles, after attempting to leave his mark on the world following the unexpected loss of his friend.

("The Legacy")

As Charles says to Caroline when he gets home, our children are our legacy. What better reminder is there, that we walked the face of this Earth, than our children?

"Once I was lost and scared and cold.
You have no family, I was told.
Except a brother to keep me warm,

In any winter or any storm.

He was as lost and scared as I,

But brave enough to never cry.

'We'll be all right,' is what he said,

'Even though Ma and Pa are dead.'

They lay in cold silence beneath the sod.

To save us would be a miracle from God.

The miracle came like a glorious dawn,

Just when it seemed all hope was gone.

The biggest thanks to God and the heavens above

For our new family's unbounded love."

A poem written by Cassandra after she and James come to live with the Ingalls.

(Uncle Jed")

I just typed that poem without looking at this episode at all. I'm not sure if it's etched in my brain so vividly because I love it so much, or because I've seen the episode 43,897 times. Probably both.

"As you can see from my dress, the wedding is off. Well, land sakes, don't look so down in the mouth! Sam and I just had a change of heart; cold feet. Anyway, there's a lot of fine food in the restaurant, and I'm in the mood for a party. So why don't you follow me?"

Hester Sue telling her wedding guests that she's broken her engagement to "Sam," a lying womanizer with a gambling and drinking problem.

("Second Chance")

It's interesting how, though we may be heartbroken by the situation, ridding ourselves of toxic people can give us the greatest peace. I, too, broke an engagement to a horrible person. It was a difficult time for me, but I ***never*** *felt so free. That decision was the best one I've ever made, and I've never regretted it for one second. Sometimes we have to take those leaps of faith when our hearts are telling us something isn't right. Don't be afraid to listen.*

"Wait a minute. Look at that. Look at that plant! I can't believe it. It's a stupid geranium! I watered it, and tended it, and splinted it when it was broken, and it just kept trying to die on me! Now look at it! A tornado hits it, and it's growing up through the ruins of the house!

You know why, Charles? It's because I over-tended it. All it needed was some time to be alone, to help itself. Just like me. As long as Laura and Eliza Jane kept doing things for me, I didn't see any reason to change."

Almanzo to Charles when he's finally decided to stop feeling sorry for himself and learn to walk again after a stroke leaves him paralyzed.

("Days of Sunshine, Days of Shadow")

I often have to remind myself to stop doing too much for my kids. If they don't learn to do things on their own, they won't develop the self-confidence they'll need to handle adulthood. They'll also get too used to not having to work hard for what they want. Independence and diligence are significant life skills that our children can only benefit from if we give them opportunities to practice them.

"I was always taught that no matter what you do to hide things from people, there's always someone who knows what you're doing."

Laura reacting to Mr. Edwards' tales about his past drinking habits.

("A Promise to Keep")

Laura and Almanzo ask him to be their daughter's godfather in this episode. They don't know that he's struggling with alcoholism, a problem that comes to a head in this story. Laura helps him through his recovery. Their bond is so special over the years.

"Louisa was my best friend, and having this baby meant everything to her. He doesn't even want this baby! Louisa's gone now. She can't save this baby, but we could!"

Caroline, suggesting that she and Dr. Baker give her friend's newborn child to a couple whose newborn has just died. Dr. Baker doesn't approve of the idea until the father of the deceased child hears the baby crying and thinks it's his own. He comes flying in and is thrilled to see the child. Dr. Baker and Caroline decide to "save" the baby and give it to the other couple.

("A Faraway Cry")

Caroline shows some spunk in this episode when her friend's husband tries to make a move on her. She smacks him, and as he comes toward her again, she picks up a lighted torch. He won't be messin' with her again!

Charles: "Isaiah, an old man came to me this morning. He talked to me. He gave James some soup. Not from the glass straw Dr. Baker gave me; Isaiah, James drank from the bowl."

Isaiah: "What's that supposed to mean?"

Charles: "That he was sent. He was, Isaiah. No mortal man can tell me otherwise."

Charles keeping extreme faith that God will save James, who has been shot.

Everyone thinks Charles is crazy until the old man visits Isaiah as well. When Caroline and Isaiah go to try to bring Charles home the next day, they find that James has been healed.

("He Was Only Twelve")

Many viewers would say that this episode is too far-fetched. I find it to be faith-filled and uplifting. I may not be in the majority, but I also believe that certain people in our lives are "sent" to us. I think God sends us many signs along our journey.

Laura: "I remember when we first moved in. I was so excited to sleep up in the loft, with

my very own window."

Charles: "Yeah, I remember it too. You were such a baby then!"

Laura: "With big, buck teeth."

Charles: "Yeah."

Laura: "You don't have to hide the tears from me, Pa."

Charles: "Good times here. Good times."

This is the first scene of season nine. The show begins with Laura's voice saying, "It was the spring of 1887. It had been a hard winter for everyone; especially for Pa. He had to sell the farm and move to where he could find work. He settled the family in Burr Oak, Iowa. Pa came back to get the last of the family's things. Pa pretended that moving on would be a great thing for the family, but I knew how much he loved the little house on Plum Creek, and I knew how much he was hurting inside.

("Times Are Changing")

Please pass the Kleenex.

"It is my duty to inform you both that we no longer live in the town of Walnut Grove."

Frustrated Laura, following a town meeting at which Harriet explains that an old bond she found entitles her to $14,000, payable by the town treasury. Since the town can't afford to pay her, she uses the bond to gain privileges for her own family.

("Welcome to Olesonville")

Great episode! A fave.

"I'm *not* Constance. I'm Laura! Laura Ingalls Wilder!"

Laura, to a deranged man who goes psycho when a business deal falls through. He shoots his wife and daughter, then wanders eerily around town. He winds up at Laura's house but thinks that she is his wife, and Jenny is their daughter.

("Rage")

I don't watch this one as much as some of the others . . . . #ScaredyCat

"If anyone has a short temper, it should be *me*. I'm not a small man. I accept your apology.

Lou Bates to Harriet, when she apologizes for her prejudice and for treating him poorly.

("Little Lou")

Lou, who has great reason to be disgusted with Harriet, chooses to make a joke and offer his forgiveness. He is **a "BIG person. A VERY big person!"**

"Excuse me, Reverend? I find this whole thing amazing. I mean a boy like Matthew can say more with his heart than most of us can ever say with our mouths. Now, yesterday, this boy was judged to be unstable; not normal. Ya see, um, I ain't had a whole lot of schoolin,' so I don't quite understand what that means. Maybe someone can explain it to me. Laura? Doc? Maybe *I'm* not normal. Judge, ya know what I wanted that boy to do yesterday? I wanted him to run away with me. He refused, because he didn't want to get his friend in trouble with the law. Maybe you can tell me, which one of us was acting normal? I mean how many of us fit that description? John, I recall you helpin' Almanzo in his field after working in your blacksmith shop all day long. A lot of people'd call you crazy for that. Good ole Nels. Two years ago, when we had the drought, you extended credit to every man in this room. Half of 'em haven't paid you back yet! That's not normal, Nels; not normal at all. How 'bout you Reverend? What do you get from all of us, besides an occasional invitation to a Sunday supper? Oh, and the right to hear all our problems! You, Doc. You took care of this boy. You gave him your best medical care. Your best! Where's the pay in that? Know what you oughta do, Doc? Just wander around this room right now, and gather up all the money everybody owes you. You don't do that, do you? You just accept a dozen eggs. Laura, do you know that you taught a wild boy how to speak with his hands?

Now that's crazy. Crazy! I'll tell you what we oughta do. We oughta take this little girl right here *(Jenny)* and we oughta send her along with Matthew. She met this boy, this unstable, this 'not normal,' this 'wild' boy, and she made a friend. A friend, Judge. Know what you oughta do? You oughta get yourself a long piece of rope and just hitch it around this whole building, and haul us all along with Matthew, because we don't act any more normal than that boy there."

Isaiah expressing his devastation after a judge rules that Matthew – a reformed "wild boy" – must be sent to an asylum.

("The Wild Boy")

I love the analogies Isaiah uses here. This writing is ***terrific.***

"Just remember: The whole secret of getting people to like you is for you to start liking yourself."

Nellie to Nasty Nancy, who has taken her place as the Oleson tyrant.

("The Return of Nellie")

This is a wonderful message for all kids to remember. What's ironic in the show is that Nancy doesn't take in a word of it. She tells Willie that she lied to Nellie about being thankful for all of her lessons. She has absolutely no intention of even ***trying*** *to be nice!*

"Walnut Grove remained the same – a quiet, country town with people who cared about each other and loved the land!"

Laura's voice at the end of an episode where the townspeople have to fight the railroad in order to avoid having it run right through their farms. It even gets to the point where the women stand up front, ready to fight. Needless to say, the citizens of Walnut Grove win.

("The Empire Builders")

I've always loved how Laura narrates the show, and it's fun to hear that "little girl" voice become the voice of a young woman as we watch adventure after adventure throughout the course of the show's ten seasons.

Isaiah: "She is a grown woman, I am a grown man, and we have a right to a life! You're just a child. What would you know about it?

Laura: "I'm the same age as Jane."

Isaiah, feeling angry that he's too old for Jane, the young woman with whom he has fallen in love.

("Love")

Being the caring guy that he is, Isaiah lets Jane go; tells her that she has her whole life ahead of her. They are both heartbroken, but deep down, they know this is the right decision.

Isaiah: "Ya know what I think? I think he's plannin' on movin' in here his-self.

Reverend Alden: "But why?!"

Isaiah: "Yeah. *Why?*"

Isaiah sharing his suspicion that the young minister who has come to Walnut Grove is scheming to take over the reverend's church.

("Alden 's Dilemma")

He ***is*** *scheming; fixing up a house for Reverend Alden, which the diocese has actually chosen to award him. Ugh, Isaiah.*

"What are ya gonna do now, go home and feel sorry for yourself? That'll do you a lot of good."

Dr. Marv, trying to get Jenny to fight back after an accident compromises her health.

("Marvin's Garden")

He encourages her to get angry and use it to her advantage; to use it to fight! My daughter used to love to watch this one over and over. I never minded, because it was a great lesson for her!

"He's my own father, and I feel poisoned by him."

Sarah, sharing with Laura her deepest feelings about her father.

("Sins of the Fathers")

One of the more difficult things we can do is stand up to our parents when we disagree with them or they hurt us. Sometimes we ***have*** *to, though. Sarah does a good job with this, and then finds the perfect way to make things right in the end.*

"That's him, Sheriff! I'll never forget that face! He's one of the Younger Brothers!"

One of three men, convinced that Isaiah is part of a wanted criminal trio. ("The Older Brothers")

This episode is similar to "The Legend of Black Jake," in terms of its semi-slapstick humor, but I don't find it nearly as funny. Definitely another chance for the show to stray from its intense plotlines.

"Beth, I knew it would be good. But I never dreamed ..."

Almanzo in amazement after Laura reads her first book to him and Jenny. ("Once Upon a Time")

This is a cool one, because it's the first that touches on Laura's pursuit of becoming a published author. As an author myself, who has worked toward the same dream since the age of eight, it's both exciting and intriguing for me to watch this episode.

"I didn't put that poison in you. You did! And you can cry, and you can beg, and you can plead, but it's not gonna work! Not with me."

Charles to Albert as he's trying to break his son of a morphine addiction. Here Albert is going through such horrible withdrawal and is begging Charles to get just a little bit of morphine from Dr. Baker.

("Home Again")

I'm sick just typing this. Addiction is so very real and serious. I pray that my children will never put themselves through something like Albert did. Life is too special to mess it up with substances that alter who God created in each of us.

Jenny: "Here's my favorite. Nathan!"

Laura: "Then everybody's gonna call him 'Nate.' How did that all get started, anyway? I mean no one ever called my pa 'Charlie,' or James 'Jimmy,' or Albert 'Al.'"

Almanzo: "Well, you never minded 'Beth.'"

Laura: "Well, that's different; because only you call me that. Besides, it's pretty. I wouldn't mind having Beth for my real first name."

Jenny: "I still think there's nothing wrong with 'Almanzo Junior.' "

Almanzo: "Well, I wouldn't mind that either, Jenny, if I was sure he was gonna be a farmer like me. But suppose he wants to be a doctor. I think he should have something more special, like 'Theodore.' "

Laura: " 'Teddy.' Everyone will call him Teddy."

Jenny: "This is getting impossible. No matter what anyone comes up with, there's always something wrong."

The Wilders trying to decide what to name their second child. They can't agree on one, so they call him "Baby Wilder."

("A Child with No Name")

This episode is happy (as the baby is born), then sad (as the baby passes away, and Laura blames Dr. Baker for his death), then even sadder (as Rose is diagnosed with Small Pox), and it finally has a happy ending (as Rose recovers and Laura apologizes to the doc). Whew!

Jason: "Ruthy, are you old?

Ruthy: "Well, what you call 'old?' "

Jason: "I don't know."

Ruthy: "Well, would you say ... your father's old?"

Jason: "Yeah, I guess he's old."

Ruthy: "Then, yes, Jason. I *am* old.

Jason: "Then ... I wanna be old too."

A very touching moment between a boy and a dying woman who has become his friend.

("The Last Summer")

You may as well keep the Kleenex out. This.Episode.Gets.Me.Every.Time. Jason is just precious, too!

"Ape, monkey ... Who cares?!?! Get rid of the thing!"

Harriet reacting to an ape that Mr. Edwards is taking care of until he can figure out where it should live permanently.

("For the Love of Blanche")

Harriet actually puts up a huge stink later in the episode, when she calls the county sheriff to have the monkey killed. She always makes things difficult, doesn't she?

"He said 'yes!' Her pa said 'YES!' "

A thrilled Willie, after he asks Rachel's father for permission to marry her.

("May I have This Dance?")

I love this episode. Willie has grown from a bratty little troublemaker to a handsome, responsible young man. He is adorable in this one! It's fun to see the early episodes when the kids are so young, compared to the later ones, after they've all grown up.

"Listen, Half-Pint, I've been doing some thinkin,' sittin' alone over at my place. The fact is, I don't wanna be alone again. Wonderin' if you've got a space here . . . if it's all right."

Isaiah, deciding to move into Laura's and Almanzo's boarding house.

("Hello and Goodbye")

Watching this episode is always strange, because it turned out to be the last regular show of the series. It ended season nine, and NBC did not renew Little House for the following fall. I always watch the episode and the actors and think, they had no idea that their show would be canceled that summer. Thank goodness NBC ran three Little House TV movies, so that Michael Landon and his cast could complete their beautiful story.

Nancy: "What's it like ... knowing you're gonna die?"

Albert: "Well, at first, I was scared ... and angry. But, ya know, once I started to think about my life, I found that I've made myself some really wonderful memories. Ya know, things I've done, all the good times, all the good friends. And ya know, the best thing about it all is that they all took place right here. And that's why I came back. 'Cause there's no better place on God's Earth. Just don't waste the time you have on it. All of you, go out.

Have a good time. Make yourself lots of good friends. Ya see that way, when it's your time to look back and find your memories, you'll see that you won't be scared or angry either."

Albert speaking to Walnut Grove's kids about living life to the fullest, after he finds out he is dying.

("Look Back to Yesterday")

One of my favorite scenes ever. I'm pretty sure I even saw my husband get teary-eyed watching this one once. It's beautiful and such a powerful reminder about the fragility of life. We can't take one minute for granted.

Nancy: "You really do hate me, don't you?"
Nels: "YESSSSSSSSSS!"

Nels has assigned spoiled Nancy the job of getting a Christmas tree, and she cuts down the pine tree in their yard. This commentary takes place between them after said tree crashes through the living room window.

("Little House: Bless All the Dear Children")

Nels cracks me up here, because Nancy's go-to line, whenever she doesn't get what she wants is, "You hate me!" Nels is always trying to convince her otherwise. So when he yells "YES" here, it is hysterical! This is also a fun side story, because the main plotline of this movie is very intense: the kidnapping of Rose and the Wilder's long journey to find her.

"Did you hear? Walnut Grove did NOT die in vain!"

Reverend Alden to all the townspeople, after they decide to blow up all the buildings in Walnut Grove when a greedy land developer proves that he owns the land on which they've built their town. ***He owns the land***, they feel, ***but what is on it is ours***.

("The Last Farewell")

*I have read that Michael Landon chose to blow up the structures on the set so that they couldn't be used in future productions. Walnut Grove was **his** town. I remember watching this movie when it aired. I sobbed at the end.*

My mother asked me, "What's wrong?"

"No more Little House," I blubbered.

"Oh, Alicia," Mom said, "Little House is going to be around for a long, long time."

I'm so glad she was right.

I've had a good life. Enough Happiness. Enough Success.
—Michael Landon

Chapter 14
My Thoughts (and Theirs!) About the Amazing Actors of the Prairie

"I've 'Taken Kindly' to 'Em!"

When you grow up watching a TV series, you feel like the characters are your friends. You feel part of their community, part of their lives. Though you know that these "people" you see on TV are fictional, you come to really love them. This love could not possibly develop if not for the incredible job that actors do, bringing their characters to life for us.

Well, I have to begin with the king. The man. The head honcho. The "Pa" of *Little House on the Prairie*. **Michael Landon.** Bear with me, because I'm going to gush here, and I didn't even know him personally. This man was beyond gifted. An actor, a writer, and a director, he was a brilliant artist who was able to imagine the extraordinary and bring it to life on screen. In one word? *Genius.* There is also no doubt that he was a family man. I think it would be impossible to create such a touching, family-oriented show without having this personal quality. Michael Landon was able to make us laugh, because he had an unbelievably contagious giggle. He made us cry, because *he* cried. Over and over again, he teared up in response to the heartwarming, sorrowful, controversial, joyous, gut-wrenching storylines he wrote. He convinced us that he was poor, hard-working, and most of all, loving. I have learned so much from him about both writing and life!

Michael Landon stood in the main spotlight along with **Karen Grassle,** who completed him in this TV series. If you've read the rest of this book, you already know that I adore her as an actress. She was amazing in this role! Her portrayal of this pioneer woman who has to be strong, disciplined, kind, skilled, friendly, wise, brave, and fun all at the same time was, ummm, outstanding. She was an 1880s SUPERHERO! Caroline Ingalls is my favorite TV mom of all time (and, believe me, I watched some good ones growing up, like Marion Cunningham, Carol Brady, Elise Keaton, and Cindy Walsh). Caroline was in a class by herself (maybe because the *Little House* **century** was in a **century** by itself). Karen Grassle was warm, gentle, sweet, convincing, feisty, firm, and wise in this role. Not easy to pull off. I remember seeing Melissa Gilbert in an interview, talking about how she idolized Karen Grassle, "who had studied." She came to *Little House* with an extensive background in theater. Her television experience wasn't as vast, but as soon as she read for Michael Landon, he sent her right to wardrobe! Karen was exceptional as Ma and became the ma we all wanted to have!

Melissa Gilbert. Wow! Clearly, she was born to play this role. She stole our hearts when she narrated her family's settlement in Walnut Grove and continued to keep us informed of their well-being over the next ten years. My childhood idol, she started out as a buck-toothed, adorable, spunky little girl and transitioned into a beautiful, wise young woman, all while on this show. She took us along on her adventures, allowing us to share in the ups and downs of Laura's life on the prairie. I've wondered how many miles she totaled over the years with all the running she did! Melissa's smile was a big one, and she played the character in a way that made us know it would be fun to be Laura's friend. I would imagine it isn't easy for child actors to grow up and make viewers see them as adults, but Melissa made this transition seamlessly and successfully. Melissa is just as wonderful in real life. I had a video chat with her about this book, and from the moment we greeted each other until the end of our conversation, I felt like I was speaking to a friend I've known for years. Melissa is kind, caring, and funny. The warmth and encouragement she has shown to me in support of this book have been amazing. She agrees that people are still watching *Little House* today because of its amazing messages and its ability to take us back to a simpler time when kindness and family love prevailed.

Melissa is a seasoned author! She has written a memoir called *Prairie Tale*, a cookbook titled *My Prairie Cookbook*, and the children's book *Daisy and Josephine*. I have read them all and thoroughly enjoyed peeking into Melissa's life on *Little House* and beyond. Check them out!

The word on the street is that there is a fourth book on the way as well!

Melissa Sue Anderson was our "Mary." In the early seasons, she played the more serious, studious character in comparison to Laura, but Melissa could also be funny and had great facial expressions! She was able to carry a very dramatic, emotional scene as well. I have a feeling that some of the storylines they gave Mary when Melissa was younger helped to prepare her for the challenging shift she had to make when it was time for her character to go blind. Let's talk about *that* episode! "I'll Be Waving as You Drive Away" was so well done, and Melissa deserved the Emmy nomination. Though I heard her say in an interview that she did become tired of playing the blind character, I really feel she made the most of it and did it so convincingly. Melissa wrote a memoir about her experiences on *Little* House *on the Prairie*. Called *The Way I See It*, the book takes us into dozens of episodes through the eyes of Melissa.

The twins who played Carrie, **Lindsay and Sidney Greenbush**, were so little when *Little House* premiered! Cute as a button. I loved when Pa found Carrie standing by the fireplace on Christmas Eve, worrying about Santa getting "all burned up" when he came down the chimney. I also think the episode "The Godsister" was cool, because both girls got to be in the show together. I read that they switched back and forth between playing Carrie and Alyssa. It was fun watching those sweet girls grow up over the years!

Baby Grace! Coming to the Ingalls family toward the end of the fourth season, she "graced" us with her presence just before Mary lost her eyesight and the family moved to Winoka. How many of us parents can imagine making *that* trip – in a covered wagon – with an infant??? Yikes! Twins **Wendi and Brenda Turnbaugh** spent four seasons on the prairie, growing from infant to toddler to little girl. Grace's arrival was a special one, because Charles delivered her, and because the scenes leading up to it were all about Caroline's need to give Charles a son. When Baby Grace arrived, Caroline was immediately enchanted and forgot all about how desperately she had wanted a son. "Oh, she's beautiful!" Caroline exclaimed.

As Grace grew, she provided many smiles for us by falling asleep in her highchair (I always figured that wasn't scripted!) and by teaming up with Charles to outsmart the other kids into making dinner for the rest of the fam.

What a fun way those twins started their "real" life – being on *Little House*! Wendi shared some interesting thoughts with me. "On the set of *Little House*, the children were everything. The way the cast and crew took care of us kids was not the norm in Hollywood. My mom didn't realize that until our first job after *Little House*. It was a one-day shoot, and they didn't know our names or if we were tired or hungry. The only thing they cared about was getting the job done as quickly as possible. Needless to say, we retired after that day . . . Nothing could compare to the family atmosphere on the set of *Little House on the Prairie*." I told Wendi that I found it remarkable, with the size of the *Little House* cast and crew, how Michael Landon was able to give such a warm, personal touch to the set. I obviously didn't know him, but it's clear that he had a huge heart and really loved his work and his "people."

Wendi is the author of a wonderful book called *A Prairie Devotional*. A beautiful collection of spiritual insights and unique memories of her days on *Little House*, Wendi's book is centered around the beauty and challenges of our everyday lives and *Little House's* themes of faith and family. I have found it to be an enlightening and comforting place to reflect on both my faith and my favorite show. A warm, kindhearted soul, it isn't surprising that Wendi created this meaningful book! She also has a great website including a blog and information about her speaking events. www.wendiloulee.com. I highly recommend!

"Oh, for Heaven's sake!" I cannot say enough about **Katherine MacGregor!** She was *absolutely phenomenal* in the role of Harriet Oleson. She knew just how to play the part so that we all loved being annoyed by her character. She was also *hilarious*! Her inflection, the various tones of voice she used, and the expressive faces she made all added up to perfection. The way she blubbered when she cried was the best. I really am shocked that Katherine didn't receive an Emmy nomination for her work on *Little House*. She added so much to the show. There's even specific music that tends to accompany her scenes (I found that with Mary, Adam, Albert, Almanzo, and dog Bandit as well)! Katherine MacGregor was totally brilliant as Harriet. Her energy, style, and timing were unmatched.

Counterpart to Harriet was good ole Nels. Such a lovable character! **Richard Bull** really owned this role. The "yes" to Harriet's "no," the truth to her lies, the voice of reason to her grandiose ideas, Nels offset Harriet beautifully. Richard Bull played the neighbor we all wanted; kind, thoughtful, and pleasant. He was someone people could rely on, in good times and bad. Richard was a great actor and was cast perfectly. I read somewhere that he was the one actor on the show whose real-life personality was most like the character he played. If that was the case, Richard must have been a joy to work with!

Alison Arngrim! Unbelievable! She *totally* rocked the part of Nellie. I feel like she got meaner as the years went on, too. She was the girl we all loved to hate! I feel as though Alison, in order to play this role, must have really had to "dig deep," because her character was *such* a piece of work. Also, I read an article about her once (I have no idea where), and its title was, "Nasty Nellie's Naturally Nice!" Knowing that she's a nice person in real life has always given me even *more* admiration for her spectacular work playing a total bitch. I love how she embraced her role, on screen and off. She has said many times in interviews that people were mean to her in public because of who she played on TV. It's always so funny to me that viewers actually think actors *are* their characters; but it happens! Alison was extremely convincing as the conniving, self-centered, terrible spoiled girl. It takes quite an actress to pull this off! Bravo!

Have you read Alison's memoir, *Confessions of a Prairie Bitch: How I Survived Nellie Oleson and Learned to Love Being Hated*? Fantastic and hilarious! A must-read.

Nellie's bratty little brother, Willie, was played by **Jonathan Gilbert** (Melissa Gilbert's real-life younger bro). As a small boy, he was really cute in this rambunctious role. Spending half his life standing in the corner at school, Willie was the kid whose mischief continuously entertained us. Jonathan literally grew up before our eyes, transforming from a tiny, messy-haired fireplug to a tall, handsome young man. His character even got married before the series ended. That episode, called "May I Have This Dance?", shows us a grown-up Willie, who is bright, responsible, kind, level-headed, and loving . . . He definitely took after Nels.

Along came Nancy. Despite Harriet's wonky parenting methods, she and Nels managed to turn out two kind, respectable kids, and then they adopted nasty Nancy. **Allison Balson** took this role and ran with it! Way meaner than Nellie ever was, Nancy was pure evil! I love the way Allison played the part. She really knew how to convince us of Nancy's spoiled, conniving spirit!

Some truly awesome work was done by **Matthew Labyorteaux**, who played Albert. Matthew was cute and appealing when his independent, sneaky character was introduced during the Ingalls' days in Winoka. As he grew during his years in Walnut Grove, he became kind, hard-working, and handsome (and still maintained some of the "sneaky," which was epic). I read somewhere that Matthew could cry on cue. This was probably a much appreciated skill on an emotional show like *Little House*. It was fun watching him join Laura and Andy to team up and get into mischief! Matthew was solid in the role of Albert.

Charles and Caroline extended their hearts and home to James and Cassandra Cooper, played by **Jason Bateman** and **Missy Francis**. These two young actors were endearing and talented (Missy, like Matthew Labyorteaux, was also a boss at crying on cue). They fit in well with the Ingalls family, and the addition of their characters created some great storylines. Missy (who now goes by **Melissa** Francis) grew up to be a journalist and works as an anchor for Fox News. She has also authored the books *Diary of a Stage Mother's Daughter* and *Lessons from the Prairie: The Surprising Secrets to Happiness, Success, and (Sometimes Just) Survival I Learned on America's Favorite Show.* And I guess we all know how successful and popular Jason Bateman is. Such a talented guy! Pretty cool that one of his first roles was on *Little House*.

Though many episodes of *Little House* were fabricated to keep entertaining the audience, much of the series stayed true to Laura Ingalls Wilder's books. One example was the inevitable introduction of Laura's husband, Almanzo. **Dean Butler** was a perfect fit! Besides having that "country boy" look, he was able to pull off the varied parts of Almanzo's (or should I say "Manly's") personality. This character was good-hearted, family-oriented, and hard-working, yet he could be as ornery and stubborn as the day is long. Dean was exceptional at portraying each and every facet of this character. Though some have said that the chemistry was poor between Laura and Almanzo, I think they got away with less lovey-dovey stuff because of the show's time period. They definitely made it work! Dean Butler clearly loved playing this role, and as a result, he convinced us of Almanzo's love for our Laura. After reading the manuscript for this book, Dean Butler told me that he enjoyed seeing the quotes from Michael Landon at the end of each chapter. The wisdom he has shared and the support he has shown to me and this project have been incredible. It's clear to me that *Little House on the Prairie* has been an extremely special part of his life. In fact, Dean has created documentaries about both the *Little House* TV show and Laura Ingalls Wilder herself. These, among other amazing *Little House*-related work done by Dean, can be found at www.Laura-Ingalls-Wilder.com. It's definitely worth a look!

A school teacher who was bright, kindhearted, friendly, *and* beautiful???? What lucky students they were in Walnut Grove to have Miss Beadle as their amazing teacher! **Charlotte Stewart** was the best choice for this balance of traits, and she did a super job inserting humor as well! Sweet as pie but firm when she needed to be, Miss Beadle was the teacher we all wanted to have.

While I was putting this book together, Charlotte was wonderfully supportive, of both the project and of me personally. She shared with me that her mother's name was Alice, and that her father often called her mom "Alicia." How fun for me to have a "name twin" in Charlotte's family! Keeping in touch with me by both email and "snail mail," Charlotte repeatedly offered her great advice and insight. One day, when I pulled a letter from her out of the mailbox, my son, John, said, "Mom, wouldn't it be funny if Miss Beadle was writing to tell you, 'This book is terrible! Go stand in the corner!' " I guess my kids have watched enough episodes to know about the dreaded corner of the Walnut Grove schoolhouse.

As it turns out, my publisher for this book, Bear Manor Media, is the same house that published Charlotte's awesome memoir, *Little House in the Hollywood Hills: A Bad Girl's Guide to Becoming Miss Beadle, Mary X, and Me.* If you're a *Little House* fan and haven't read it, I suggest you get a copy and cozy up. You'll love it!

Did you know that Charlotte also makes and sells "Miss Beadle Bags?" These beautiful, patchwork tote bags are made with pretty fabric patterns chosen by Charlotte. The best part? Each bag has a photo from *Little House* on it! I just love mine and can't wait to "tote" my books around in it when I go to signing events!

"No peekin!' Can't stand for no peekin!' " Our beloved Mr. Edwards. Always good for a smile and a chuckle. The casting directors couldn't have chosen a better actor for this role than **Victor French.** His character was a real, what-you-see-is-what-you-get kind of guy. Who doesn't love someone real? From the pilot episode when he taught Laura to spit to the very last TV movie when Mr. Edwards led Walnut Grove's fight against the land developer, Victor French made us giggle, cry, and think over the years. His character had a lot to say, and, for someone who didn't have much schoolin,' he taught us so much.

Who could better balance Mr. Edwards than the sweet, easy-going, friendly, spunky Grace Snyder? **Bonnie Bartlett** did a wonderful job playing the widow who "took to" Mr. Edwards right away and patiently waited for him to notice her. Then, when a neighbor passed away leaving her three children without parents, Grace stepped in to care for them. I love how Bonnie Bartlett convinced us of her character's love for those children! I also love that Mr.

Edwards finally woke up and married Grace! When I asked Bonnie Bartlett about her experiences on the show, she said, "I loved working on *Little House*. Michael was a good producer. But I must stress – getting into costume and the period, which I loved, was not a complete reality. It was a bit of a western fairy tale. I've always loved fairy tales, and they often are lessons. So I guess that is the best way to describe *Little House*! It taught lessons for children and sometimes adults. On my part, I had so much fun doing the lighter stuff, and then the more serious scenes that all that humor and fun also taught."

I agree with Bonnie; *Little House* ***was*** like a fairy-tale, in so many ways, for so many people.

When the three children were orphaned in the emotional episode "Remember Me," they were cared for and eventually adopted by Isaiah and Grace. **Radames Pera** played the oldest child, "John, Jr." The rather handsome Radames gave a memorable performance in this story, successfully portraying his extremely vulnerable yet insanely strong character. He told me that this is one of his favorite episodes, because he got to work with Patricia Neal, the Hollywood legend. "In the second half of that two-parter, I always burst out crying whenever I watch the scene where Victor French's character decides he can't live with breaking up the three kids into two separate homes and decides to propose *(to Grace)* and adopt them all. What a fine tear-jerker there!"

Radames shared his feelings about what he has gained from his *Little House* experience: "I can only say that I feel incredibly lucky to have been in this show. The friendships I have been able to have, initiated by Michael, were largely expanded upon and precipitated by Alison Arngrim, whom I knew in high school and whom is a dear friend today; Charlotte Stewart, whom I love so much; the genuine connections I feel with Dean Butler, Melissa

Gilbert, Hersha Parady, Rachel Greenbush Sanchez, and more recently with Pam Roylance and Dave Friedman (as a result of the fan events we've been able to spend time around each other because of). Each of these people is a blessing in my life in their own way. Lucky and very grateful."

Radames appreciates the fan events and the opportunities they have provided. "Were it not for the legacy of *Little House*, being a somewhat "bi-coastal American" . . . I would never know other parts of the great nation of America; nor France, the country I now call 'home' and where I met my wife, who became the mother of our beautiful child! Just goes to show that you never know where something will lead."

I have found Radames to be much like his character, John, Jr. He's friendly, pleasant, and thought-filled. After sharing with me his detailed reflections of his *Little House* cast mates and experiences, he wished me luck with this book and thanked me for asking him to contribute, adding, "It's a genuine honor." Believe me, Radames, the honor is all mine. Thank *you*.

John, Jr. had two siblings. "Carl" was played by **Brian Part**. His character was curious and playful, always trying to be like his adoptive pa, Isaiah. Brian was great! The sweet little sister, "Alicia," was portrayed by **Kyle Richards**. This brown-eyed cutie stole our hearts in "Remember Me" and continued to play the role of Alicia for several years. Kyle's sister, Kim Richards, also appeared on *Little House* as Olga in the episode "Town Party, Country Party." Talented siblings!

The Garvey Family! Going through the trials and tribulations of life in both Walnut Grove and Winoka alongside the Ingalls, the Garveys were not only their neighbors but true friends. **Merlin Oleson** was as tall and broad as they come, but he knew how to play the loving man just as well as the strong farmer. Merlin made the transition from professional football player to actor exceptionally well. He was so loved in the role of Jonathan.

Hersha Parady was a fan fave with her lively but gentle way of portraying Alice. Her character was one that most women would want to have as a friend, in any time period. It's no wonder so many of us were crushed when she was killed in that fire at the blind school. I have to tell you, also, that Hersha is just as wonderful in person. Her endearing warmth and fabulous sense of humor make her friendly and fun. She has fond memories of her time on *Little House* (and was disappointed when her character was killed off). Hersha told me, "The quality of the whole show was wonderful. From the direction, to the actors, guest stars, writers, costumes, and cinematography, it was wonderful. And the production quality was amazing. Once you worked on *Little House on the Prairie*, it was hard for any other set to compare."

When I asked her what she most admired about Michael Landon, Hersha had a list! "He was brilliant. He really knew how to evoke emotion. I loved his sense of humor! But the greatest was his humility. He didn't see himself as the Hollywood heartthrob. In fact, he kind of made fun of the idea of himself as a star." Hersha is just as down-to-earth herself. She's delightful!

The part of Andy Garvey was played by the talented **Patrick Labyorteaux,** whose character got into all kinds of fun and mischief (and even some danger) with Laura and Albert over the years. Patrick Labyorteaux not only touched our hearts in this role, but has gone on to do some really great work as an adult actor, too!

The Carter family was introduced to us at the start *Little House's* ninth season, at which time the show's name was changed to *Little House: A New Beginning*. John, Sarah, Jeb, and Jason Carter were a wonderful addition to Walnut Grove. It's a good thing, because they "replaced" the Ingalls family when Charles and Caroline decided to move to Iowa. It was strange at first to see a different family living in the little house, but the Carters quickly won us over.

John Carter was played by **Stan Ivar**, who had the big job of portraying a Charles-like character. Strong yet sensitive, firm but fun, and always the gentleman, John was very likeable. I think Stan Ivar filled Charles' shoes quite nicely!

Pamela Roylance was a teacher in Oregon when she decided to head to Los Angeles and act. *Little House* was on her wish list of shows. Smart woman, and what an ideal fit she was! Pamela portrayed the kind, loving, intelligent Sarah Carter in a way that just drew us right in! The casting directors made the perfect choice! After all, Sarah was "the new Caroline" in a sense. Talk about big shoes to fill! Well, Pamela nailed it. I would imagine that the part came somewhat naturally to her. You know how Pamela played a good-hearted, gentle character with a great sense of humor? Well, I'm here to tell you that Pam is just as delightful in real life! In an hour-long interview, she shared stories with me of her *Little House* days as well as her life before and after she played Sarah Carter. She wanted to hear all about me and my life as well. Pam and I discovered that we share a desire to treat others with kindness and to smile easily. We discussed how this "*Little House* value" is so very important today. Talking about wearing masks during this Covid-19 pandemic, Pam and I giggled because both of us hate that no one can see us smiling with those things on! "I try to scrunch my eyes up so they know I'm smiling under there!" Pam said. She told me that she loved working on *Little House* and with Michael Landon. "He was so thorough with his thoughts and his vision," she said. One of her funny memories has to do with Michael Landon's incredible sense of humor. "When one of us was supposed to walk away into the distance at the end of a scene, Mike would only whisper, 'Cut' to the cameramen and crew. So the person would be walking and walking, wondering when the scene would be over. One time, I was walking with Melissa Gilbert, and *she* knew the gig. We walked for a bit, and then she said, 'Pam, we are going to turn around, and everyone will be laughing at us.' Sure enough, Melissa was right. They were all laughing! Melissa said to me, 'You're initiated into the group!' " I loved hearing this story about the fun that cast members had behind-the-scenes!

Jeb Carter was played by **Lindsay Kennedy**. He was the perfect big brother. Teasing and deceiving, being bossy, and then turning around and looking out for his little brother on the flip side made Jeb a cool guy. It was interesting to see how much Lindsay grew and changed in height and look during the two years he was involved in *Little House.* He made a great Jeb!

David Friedman portrayed the adorable Jason Carter. This kid could melt your heart with one smile! His character was spunky and fun, yet sweet and sensitive. David did it all so well. Today, he enjoys participating in cast events and reunions. He looks back fondly on his *Little House* experience. He told me, "I think the thing that makes me most proud of being part of *Little House on the Prairie* was the fact that I was part of American pop culture and TV history. I didn't realize the impact of the show internationally until I participated in the *Little House on the Prairie* cast reunion in Walnut Grove, Minnesota, in July of 2019. I was flattered to be a part of that event, and to say that I got a kick out of it is an understatement! I had a great time reuniting with the cast and was touched by the passion and love of the fans."

When I spoke with Dave, he was friendly, funny, and just as interested in hearing about me as he was in talking about *Little House*. When I told him I'm from the Philadelphia area, he immediately asked me, "Geno's or Pat's?" For those of you who aren't from this part of the country, Dave was referring to two rivaling Philly cheesesteak stands! Good stuff. Great guy.

There's a unique camaraderie between the members of the *Little House* cast, even after nearly fifty years. Clearly, their experiences on the set were positive and special. The seeds of love that Michael Landon obviously "planted" truly yielded a "harvest" of amazing relationships and unbreakable bonds.

I came home and found my 12-year-old daughter devouring the Laura Ingalls Wilder books. Then I discovered that my wife had devoured them too and was reading them again. So I went to NBC and told them "Little House" was it.

—Michael Landon

Chapter 15
My Little House Story
"V.I.P. Treatment?!?!?!"

Little House on the Prairie has been a favorite of mine since I was a little girl. I just turned fifty, and the show first aired when I was three years old, so it's basically been a happy part of my *entire* life. Everyone has a favorite TV show. This one is special to me, because I feel I learned and benefitted from its lessons as a child and am now seeing those lessons from a parent's perspective and learning *new* things from them.

I grew up on Long Island, and my parents were friendly with a couple named Kevin and Carole O'Sullivan. Mr. O'Sullivan was the president of Worldvision Enterprises, which distributed *Little House on the Prairie* on behalf of NBC. Mr. O'Sullivan also executive produced Michael Landon's film, *Sam's Son* (1984).

I remember going to the O'Sullivans' home for dinner with my parents and saying in awe, "You know Michael Landon???"

Mr. O'Sullivan responded with a laugh, "No, Michael Landon knows ***me***!" He also told us that sometimes, when he called Michael Landon on the phone, his daughter (age three at the time) would ask to speak to him.

"Hello, Pa?" Mr. O's daughter would say.

Michael Landon would happily chat with her.

"Where are Mary and Laura?" she'd ask.

"Well, they're asleep in their beds," he would tell her.

Even though I knew he was a fictional character, I remember thinking it was so cool that this three-year-old got to talk to "Pa" on the telephone. In real life, Michael Landon obviously created the same magic for children that Pa did. According to the O'Sullivans, he was wonderful with his fans as well; gracious and warm, happy to greet them and sign autographs if asked. Mrs. O. would comment on Michael's endearing laugh and, of course, his good looks.

At age eleven, I wanted to send Melissa Gilbert a letter. The O'Sullivans requested that I write it and give it to them; they would get it to Michael Landon's secretary, who would be instructed to give it to Melissa personally. WOW! Mrs. O'Sullivan invited my mom and me over to their house for lunch on the day I would give them my letter, and she gave me *The Little House Cookbook* as a gift. It was so kind. I felt so special . . . I also felt like *I* should be showering *her* with gifts for delivering my letter to my favorite actress!

The following year (1983), my dad had business in California and decided we should all go as a family. It was a wonderful trip during which we visited San Francisco, San Diego, and Los Angeles. When we got to L.A., I asked my mom if there was any way we could go to the *Little House* set. She wasn't sure where it was and how all of that worked. I begged her to call Mrs. O'Sullivan and ask. Mom said she didn't feel comfortable doing that. I was bummed.

After we got home, my mom told Mrs. O'Sullivan how I'd pleaded with her to try to find out how to visit the set. Mrs. O'Sullivan said, "Oh, you should have called me! We could have set that up! They would've taken you on a tour of the whole thing, and you would have gotten VIP treatment, too." My mom should NEVER have told me that. I've never let her live it down, especially because the show ended soon afterward; and even in Simi Valley, the "Walnut Grove" buildings were blown up in the series finale. I knew that I'd never get a chance to go see them.

In April of 1991, the world learned that Michael Landon had been diagnosed with inoperable pancreatic cancer. Again, I picked up my pen and started to write a letter. I wanted to tell him I hoped he was doing okay, wish him well with his treatment, and encourage him to fight. "I haven't met you yet!" I wrote. I included quotes from Little House, like "Keep the horseshoe hung over the door" and "Onward, Christian Soldier" (although I aware he wasn't Christian, I felt he'd "get it"). I don't know if he ever received my letter (probably not; he said in an interview that there were hundreds of thousands), but I was glad I had sent it.

On July 1, 1991, my mom came to me in the kitchen as I made myself a snack. "I have something to tell you," she said. "... Michael Landon passed away today."

"Oh, don't tell me that," I answered quietly as tears blurred my eyes. He was gone.

Remember me with smiles and laughter, for that is how I will remember you all.
If you can only remember me with tears, then don't remember me at all.
—Michael Landon

Chapter 16
Quarantine

Fears, Tears and Little House Years

THIS CHAPTER WASN'T PART OF MY ORIGINAL MANUSCRIPT.

The first scratchings of this project were positive parenting notes I made for myself as I watched and reflected on *Little House* during the Covid lockdown of spring 2020. Realizing that this made me happy in a somewhat unhappy time period, I felt that others may find joy in it, too. From there, a book poured out of my mind and through my fingers over the months that followed, and I was thrilled with the outcome!

Fast forward to the year anniversary of the shutdown. On March 13, 2021, I tested positive for Covid. Huh??? I had masked! I had distanced! I had been cautious! But I got it.

In an instant (at the sight of that test result), I was isolated in my bedroom, away from my husband, my children – and basically my life – for two weeks.

Though I felt sick, I chose to make that time of quarantine a time to be as productive as I could be under the circumstances. Having uninterrupted time to proofread this book, I tweaked and revised, and added, and edited . . . and watched a good amount of *Little House* on TV. Now, trust me – I have easily seen each episode 87-and-a-half million times over the last 46 years. This time, however, I was seeing them with different eyes.

As I looked at my life while lying in bed, I began to make decisions and plans about how I would be different – better – when I could eventually emerge from the confinement of my room. I also began to ingest the rich messages of *Little House* with new urgency and understanding. The life lessons and positive values I've always cherished now had even greater meaning. I felt a personal connection to the hopes and ideals that Michael Landon held dear. He wanted his viewers to love life and to love themselves. He aspired to spread joy through his stories about family and community. And, boy, did he succeed!

Michael Landon knew how to get to the core of our emotions and make us think. As a boy, he was terribly mistreated by his mother. When he became an adult, he chose to take that awful experience and create uplifting family television for people everywhere. His oldest daughter was in a devastating car accident and nearly lost her life. As he sat at her bedside, Michael made a deal with God: If He would let her live, Michael promised to spend his life doing something meaningful that would leave the world a better place than he'd found it.

We learn by Michael's example that there are always choices in life. We always have the option to rise above adversity, take the high road, do the right thing, choose goodness, and make a difference.

My case of Covid was what I'd call a "medium case." I had a sore throat, headache, stomachache, cough, runny nose, and achiness in my legs and arms. I felt so blessed, however, that there were no respiratory issues and that I was at home instead of in a hospital. There was one day that I experienced shortness of breath, but my oxygen level tested fine. I'm sure it was just anxiety, but it alarmed me. Having Covid definitely made me feel scared in general. At the risk of sounding overly dramatic, it was frightening to be in the grip of this virus that has taken so many lives. I'd heard about a friend of a friend who, at my age, contracted Covid, exhibited my same symptoms at first, and then suddenly had trouble breathing and, within a few weeks, passed away. Young guy, no underlying health conditions, no risk factors; but Covid took him. I couldn't get this scenario out of my mind. How did I know that the same thing wouldn't happen to me?

Michael Landon's words, *"Whatever you want to do, do it now. There are only so many tomorrows"* really resonated with me while I was sick. It's so easy to put things off – even important things – because our lives become so busy with other "stuff." Michael's sudden, short but terminal illness and death in 1991 are a billboard advertisement for his message to us. It's *never* too soon to tackle a goal, wrong a right, realize a dream, mend a difference, or blaze a new trail. The time to love – and to live – is ***now***.

Like Michael after his childhood, and like his daughter after her accident, we sometimes are blessed with the gift of a second chance. Even though my bout with Covid didn't threaten or take my life, I recognize that I am truly lucky, because it very well could have. That being true, I consider my recovery to be a second chance. Before me – before each of us – lies the road to the future. It's paved with endless possibility and opportunity. As I walk down *my* road, I plan to heed Michael's advice, live by his example, and be my very best self.

Whatever you want to do, do it now. There are only so many tomorrows.
—Michael Landon

Chapter 17
For Michael Landon

"I'm Much Obliged."

Dear Mr. Landon,

It's been thirty years since you left this earth. *So* hard to believe; but oh, what you left behind! A timeless legacy. A work of art. An example of pure genius. *Little House on the Prairie.* The way you poured yourself into this series is evident. The writing, acting, and direction are brilliant. As a writer myself, I have learned a great deal from your wisdom and style. As a person, I have internalized the countless values and lessons that *Little House* has gifted to me and to all of your viewers. Thank you for those!

The members of your amazing cast adored you. I love when Melissa Gilbert refers to you as "my pa." She clearly learned so much from you and was shaped by your example. When asked about you, Melissa has said, "He believed that people are always really good at heart, and that anyone is redeemable, and that the only way to change things is to do it from a place of love, and fairness, and understanding." You really left a footprint on Melissa's heart; and on the hearts of millions.

It sounds like you exuded the warmth of a father to all of the children in your cast. Wendi Lou Lee told me, "I remember, as a very young child, thinking that Michael Landon was my dad. He brought a calming, fatherly presence into my life that I didn't have at home until my mom remarried a few years after *Little House* ended. It was quite confusing for me when he didn't come home for dinner, but days on the set unfolded like a dream. Toddlers don't exactly understand the whole acting gig, especially at two years old. You could say that Michael Landon, as a father figure, set the bar high."

Dean Butler told me, "He was a gifted man who shared his tender, vulnerable heart so generously with his audience." Clearly, Dean understood and respected you deeply.

Because my crazed *Little House* fandom has spanned my entire lifetime, I have watched and read almost all of the interviews out there about you and your amazing career. Between these and the personal interactions I've had with *Little House* cast members, one thing is consistent: everyone talks about your incredible way of promoting family values. The young people in your cast recall how well you related to kids and how you created a safe place for them. They trusted you because you were always approachable, available, and accessible. They felt they could talk to you about anything, because of the way you welcomed them in. While the adults (cast and crew alike) speak about your brilliance as a writer, director, actor, and producer, they all seem to mention how you made them feel like part of a family. *Your TV family*.

Pamela Roylance told me, "I loved working with Michael and felt lucky to be part of his cast. He encouraged everyone to get along and to believe in themselves. Mike would tell us, 'Don't believe what the press says about you.' He was always loving and warm, allowing guests to visit the set and greeting them personally. Mike was very generous with the cast and crew as well. He would give us a catalog at the holidays and let us pick out any gift. He wanted us to have something we really wanted."

Radames Pera recalls all of your amazing facets: "I remember Michael in several ways; as a boss, as a fellow actor, as an "actor's director," and as a workaholic. As The Boss, I and everyone else knew that he was in charge, and he knew how to wield that power well, for the most part. He expected everyone to bring their A-Game every day, and that was an appropriate expectation; we're in a very costly situation, all of us, and we're there to do one thing: deliver our maximum effort without complaint or excuses. This is perhaps even more poignant, and pointed, for child actors, for, among other things, we are all highly trained people-pleasers, we know that our longevity in The Biz, and our next job is completely dependent on "delivering the goods" as well as being a good team player."

"As a fellow actor," Radames shared, "he was great to work opposite. Present, generous, authentic, deep. He made us all look our best . . . He gave each actor what they needed to do their best, and we all gave back a 100% in return. He got things done quickly (a huge asset in TV production), because he held his team together so well . . . He made it as pleasant as one can, by hiring goodhearted people. Though we all knew we were there to work hard, the "vibe" was a generally healthy one; as healthy as a TV set in the middle of Hollywood can be, I reckon."

Dave Friedman shared a humorous memory of you. "While I was only nine and ten years old when I was on the show, I do feel like I knew Michael well. One notable memory I have is when I stayed the weekend at his Malibu house with some of his kids. I recall it feeling very comfortable and 'normal.' After a day of swimming in his pool, I remember going to the grocery store to get snacks, because we were all going to watch movies later that night. Well, as we were walking through the store, I accidentally burped. I was embarrassed and, of course, apologized immediately. Michael replied with something to the tune of, 'Oh, come on! You could do better than that.' Well, what he didn't know was that I had a keen talent of being able to burp (loudly) on command. I then let a good one rip, and he countered. There I was, walking through the grocery store in Malibu burping with Michael Landon!"

When asked about you in a television interview on *Today* (2014), Karen Grassle expressed her joy about the longevity of *Little House on the Prairie's* popularity and said that she wished you could see what it still means to people. I hope you can, too! *Little House* is still on TV all over the world every single day, and people are loving it as much today as they always have (even more so, as we try to navigate our "new normal" during this very strange time of global pandemic). I read somewhere that you had once said you believed that long after you were gone, your shows would still be on the air, touching people's lives. You were right. A fourth generation of fans is benefitting from the wisdom you imparted in your writing. What a profound accomplishment, and what an extraordinary gift you gave to the world! A big thank you for creating a legacy that has touched my life in a beautiful way. I hope that *my* writing can somehow give this same kind of joy to others.

"Much Obliged,"
Alicia

Acknowledgements

THIS PROJECT, WHICH BEGAN IN MY HEART as simple "comfort writing" about my all-time favorite TV show during the lockdown of a pandemic, grew into a work of both passion and pride as I kept daring myself to "take it a step further" until I somehow turned it into a book that was receiving enthusiasm and praise from those closest to the *Little House* series itself.

I'd like to say thank you my kick-ass husband, Jack, for his unbelievable support and for sharing in my excitement as this all unfolded. Thank you to my children, John, Colleen, and Brendan, who – though they're *so* over my being an author (because it hasn't made me rich or famous . . . yet) – have embraced the constant presence of *Little House* on our TV and have understood that this book means a lot to me. Thanks also to Mom and Dad, Bill and Karen for cheering me on!

Thank you, Ben Ohmart, for your *"Great-looking book! Let's do it!"* acceptance of my manuscript, and for sharing my belief that the 30th anniversary of Michael Landon's passing is an important anniversary and a monumental reason to honor him with this work. Thanks so much for your help and advice along the way!

To Lili Rosenstreich – Your talent and ability to "work magic" are unmatched. Thank you for your creativity, insight, and never-ending patience! xoxoxo

Trip Friendly, your constant acceptance, support, enthusiasm, and warm welcome to me and this project have been remarkable. I am truly grateful for your wisdom and guidance, and I thank you endlessly for believing in this book.

Thank you, Dean Butler! You have been unbelievably helpful and encouraging. I can't express my gratitude enough. From start to finish, you were willing to provide whatever assistance you could. I am endlessly thankful.

Hersha Parady! My warmest thanks for *your* warm welcome when I presented this project idea to you. Your enthusiasm about the timeliness of this book reinforced my need to write it. Your insight, advice, and amazing energy have enhanced my love of this iconic show and of you as an actress. Thank you for embracing me and this project the way you did!

Many, many thanks, Charlotte Stewart, for taking me under your wing during this whole process and guiding me with more knowledge and support than you probably even know. I am forever grateful. Xoxoxo

Melissa Gilbert, thank you for your amazing contributions and insight. The interest and encouragement you have given me are unforgettable, and, needless to say, so was the opportunity to meet and speak with you! Thank you from the bottom of my heart.

My sincere thanks to Wendi Lou Lee . . . You are wonderful! I thank you for embracing this project with such warmth. I am proud to say we're fellow authors!

Pam Roylance, it was an honor to speak with you and hear all about your life before and after *Little House*! You are a gem, and I appreciate your contributions more than I can express.

To Dave Friedman, who knew that the Pat's/Geno's thing was "a thing!" Your friendly welcome into the *Little House* world and your excitement for me when you learned I was pursuing this project will never be forgotten. Thank you so much for participating!

Thanks, Radames Pera. Your interest and willingness to take part in this project are warmly received. I value your time and contributions more than you know!

Todd Bridges! The passion with which you responded to my inquiry about *Little House* was completely gratifying, because you immediately understood where I was going with this book. You took hold of the messages I wanted to emphasize and poured out your innermost feelings about them. You know how relevant the *Little House* values are – even today – and you are willing to speak to their importance. Thank you, Todd.

Bonnie Bartlett, thank you for your immediate willingness to hear about this project and for the thoughts and memories you shared so openly. Your contributions are met with great appreciation!

Thank you also to Jen Delaney, Allan Duffin, Andy Demsky, Brad Lemack, Patrick Labyorteaux, Alison Arngrim, Getty Images, NBC Universal, WGA, Little House Heritage Trust, Noel Silverman, Margarita Wallach, Jim Freebery, and Sean Hayes. I couldn't have done it without your help and support!

Lilyanna, Evy, Lily, Tommy, and Abby . . . You're famous! Thank you for loving *Little House* and for being part of my book!

With Love,

Alicia

www.ingramcontent.com/pod-product-compliance
Lightning Source LLC
LaVergne TN
LVHW010936100826
845153LV00001B/64
9781629337593